THE LIFE STORY OF
BOOKER T. WASHINGTON

FROM SLAVE TO COLLEGE PRESIDENT

THE LIFE STORY OF
BOOKER T. WASHINGTON

FROM SLAVE TO COLLEGE PRESIDENT

G. HOLDEN PIKE

WILDSIDE PRESS

**THE LIFE STORY OF BOOKER T. WASHINGTON:
FROM SLAVE TO COLLEGE PRESIDENT**

Published in 2009 by Wildside Press.
www.wildsidepress.com

CHAPTER I

WANTED: A MAN—THE MAN FOUND

Just at the most severe crisis of the war between France and Germany, over thirty years ago, a London newspaper, in describing the situation, remarked that France wanted not men, but a Man. During a whole generation which followed after the close of the gigantic and sanguinary conflict between the Northern and Southern States of the American Republic, a similar remark would have applied to the millions of slaves who, though nominally free, were drifting hither and thither, now groping in the wrong direction altogether, or missing opportunities they might have embraced, had there but been one commanding personality in their midst to give the word and lead the way. There seemed to be too many negroes, while they were still increasing with a rapidity which inspired misgiving. The race seemed to be "at sea" for want of a Man. At length the much-needed chief or leader was found in Booker T. Washington, whose distinguished work on behalf of the race at the great institution which he has founded at Tuskegee has given him a world-wide reputation. As a negro, his mission is to the men and women of his own nation.

In regard to this man with his commanding personality, the *International Monthly* of New York says: — "At the present time he is universally recognised as the foremost representative of his race. He is eagerly sought after as a speaker. Whatever he chooses to write immediately finds a willing publisher. Newspaper eulogy declares him to be a remarkable orator. He is often spoken of as of solid, and even brilliant, intellectual attainments. How much of all this vogue and of this unusual reputation is based upon the fact that he is a negro, and how much upon his native merit when weighed and judged without regard to any other consideration whatsoever? Has he, in fact, done that which, had he been a white man, would have given him a solid and substantial claim to the esteem that he now enjoys?"

Mr Harry T. Peck, who writes thus, ventures the opinion that the estimate of the public in regard to Booker Washington is exaggerated. "There is no evidence that his mind is in any way exceptional," he adds. . . . "Were he a white man, he never would be singled out for eminence. . . . He is not an orator; he is not a writer; he is not a thinker. He is something more than these. He is the man who comes at the psychological moment and does the thing which is wanting to be done, and which no one else has yet accomplished." This can hardly be accepted as genuine criticism. Just as we judge a tree by its fruits, so we measure capacity, and even genius, by its results. If, as is generally acknowledged to be the case, Booker Washington has practically solved that Race Problem which American politicians have hardly dared to face since the close of the Civil War, it is only fair that we accord him the distinction of possessing that original shrewdness which may even be called genius. When an idea of exceptional value is given forth, one that is all the greater on account of its simplicity, people seem to be naturally disposed to underrate the power which gave it utterance. Booker Washington may merely be following in the footsteps of Adam Smith when, instead of regarding the negro population as an evil or a grievance, he prescribes that their labour, as a source of vast wealth, be utilised for the national advancement. Viewed from any other standpoint, there can be no doubt that the rapidly-increasing negroes inspire some disquieting apprehensions as a possible source of inconvenience or of actual danger. Once get the coloured race well under control, however, and the result would be all-round satisfaction.

Thus Booker Washington is not only the man of the hour to his own people; in him the Man who has been wanted for forty years has been found. Being somewhat over forty years of age, he was born in those portentous times towards the end of the sixth decade of the last century when the political horizon of the Republic was darkening and showing symptoms of the coming Civil War. Virginia, his native State, was the most populous and wealthy of the original thirteen, which, as colonies, separated from Great Britain after the War of Independence. In the days of his childhood, before the Civil War actually broke out, his surroundings were those of the cabin standing amid the squalor of slavery. All the sad, as well as the comic, phases of life on the Southern plantations, as they then existed, are vividly remembered by Booker Washington. Of course, to the slaves themselves very much depended on the disposition of their owners, or on the character of the overseers which those planters employed. The lot of Booker Washington was what may be called an average one. It was not so bad as that of many others who were less fortunate; nor was it so good as the exceptional experience of the few who were born amid the most favourable surroundings. It was, of course, a sad childhood, unrelieved by anything like what we should in Great Britain call the comforts of life. He was a keen-witted lad; but the shrewdest of seers could not have foreseen that he would develop into the man of hope whom the negroes, after their coming emancipation, would most sorely need.

At the time of his birth, some forty-three or forty-four years ago — the exact place or time being alike unknown — the public sentiment in regard to emancipation had made great advances, and this had been effected chiefly through the diffusion of millions of copies of Mrs H. B. Stowe's *Uncle Tom's Cabin*. Among those in this country who believed the descriptions in that work to be exaggerated, and that Legree was a non-existent character, we have to include Charles Dickens. At the same time, that famous novelist, in common with some others, probably clearly saw that the days of slavery were numbered. "In truth, it must be so," remarked one journalist at the time when *Uncle Tom's Cabin* was the most popular book both in the Old and the New World. "In truth, it must be so, for the very laws of population forbid the permanence of slavery in America. The black man thrives where the white man decays, and it is the knowledge of this very remarkable fact that in great part accounts for the dislike to the coloured population which is everywhere expressed in the United States." The social inequality of the negroes and the whites struck people then, as it does today in this country, as being one of the most marked features of American society. There is probably no remedy for that state of things, and it is partly through his recognising this fact, and knowing that the negroes must continue to be a race by themselves, that Booker Washington's success has been what it is.

Meanwhile, what kind of existence was the everyday life on a plantation "down South" in the days of Booker Washington's childhood? By way of reply, take this vivid word-picture from Mr Casey's *Two Years on the Farm of Uncle Sam*, which was published in the decade of our hero's birth: —

"The slaves are all that I had imagined, coming up to the dark outline of fancy with a terrible precision. We put in to wood at one of these places, and for the first time I saw these hewers of wood and drawers of water. A party of us went on shore to shoot; some distance in the wood we found two men, three women and two boys; there were twenty in all on this farm. The women were dressed in a rough, shapeless, coarse garment, buttoned at the back, with a sort of trousers of the same material, rough shoes and stockings, the upper garment reaching nearly to the ankle; a kind of cloth, like a dirty towel, was wound round the head. One of the women drove an ox-team; she had a large and powerful whip, with which, and a surprising strength, she belaboured and tugged the unwieldy team with great dexterity. The other woman had five children, and assisted in loading the wood; the younger, about sixteen years of age, had one child, and appeared to do nothing. The women, it seemed to me, worked harder than the men. I observed the almost complete absence of memory in the elder woman; she could not remember where she had left the link-chain or goad-whip, though but a few minutes out of her hand. I must confess that, looking on that labour-crooked group, I felt a dislike, strong and definite, to that system which takes away even the hope of improvement, crushing down the principle of self-esteem in the man, until it reaches the passive and unambitious existence of the oxen which he drives. And looking on those women, negroes though they were, so unnaturally masculine, so completely unsexed, so far removed from all those attributes with which the name of woman is associated, I felt that no reason based on an asserted right, no fiction of argument, could stand in my judgment but as dust in the balance when the question is whether a human being — no matter of what colour, whether an Indian or an African sun may have burned upon him — should possess the liberty or right of securing his own happiness to the extent of his ability. Then their state, their look, bodies, mind and manner were so many self-evident arguments against the system, which no representations, however plausible, could refute; and all that I had listened to from Southerners on the voyage disappeared like gossamer in the tempest before the mute, living picture of wretchedness presented by that group."

Brought up amid such surroundings, one would not know much about his ancestry, if anything at all. A great planter gave no more heed to the pedigree of his slaves than he did to that of his cattle; all alike were bought and sold in the open market, and neither one nor the other had any rights or privileges apart from the will of their owners. The cabin of the slave family was, in a very literal sense, what its name implied — a cabin and nothing more. The household was not supposed to need more than one room; the furniture was, of course, as rude as the hovel itself, and, though the apartment would be well ventilated, glass windows were not considered necessary. A pallet on the earthern floor was the only sleeping accommodation. It was one-room life under one of its worst phases; and, in addition to other drawbacks, the inmates suffered from cold and draughts in winter and from heat in summer. It is almost needless to say that under such conditions and amid such surroundings a lad like Booker Washington fared neither better nor worse than tens of thousands of his fellows; his earliest days were not cheered by any of the sunshine of childhood. As a rule, the children of the slave-cabin knew nothing of those ordinary sports and pastimes which relieve and give variety to the early days of the young under happier circumstances. Of course, he was not more than a child when slavery came to an end, but in the case of such a child slave, at a very early age indeed, his possible service was found to be commercially too valuable to be altogether dispensed with. He could do duty as a messenger or as a porter between the great house — a sumptuous palace in comparison with the slave-cabins — and the fields where his elders were at work. With a horse he could also go on more distant errands, some of which, along lonely roads, were not unattended with danger. Thus the dense, dark woods through which he might have to pass, when taking corn to be ground at a distant mill, would be haunted by imaginary spectres; and, besides, there were said to be deserters from the Confederate Army hidden in those recesses who, by way of sport, would relieve any negro lad of his ears if they chanced to meet with him. Such were the last repellent phases of that phase of that now obsolete world of slavery in Old Virginia as Booker Washington remembers them.

In our common, everyday talk we are accustomed to say that the darkest hour of night precedes the dawn of day. It was so in this instance. The time of Booker Washington's birth, and for some years after, was apparently the darkest period in the history of the slaves of the Southern States. For long the negroes of the plantations not only grew up quite illiterate — it was a punishable offence for them to make any endeavour to learn to read, or for anyone to attempt to teach them. Not very long before the Fugitive Slave Law had found a place in the Statute Book of the Republic, and this Act made it illegal for any fugitive slave to find either shelter or aid in any State of the Union. Then, just about the same time, the American Chief-Justice had, in his official capacity, declared that nowhere in any one of the States had a slave any rights of citizenship. In a word, the slaves on a plantation were simply on a level, in a legal sense, with the cattle they tended or used in their everyday work. For example, the mere children had no regular meal times in the conventional sense as we understand things; and there was little or nothing of what we should recognise as family life. Thus when, after the era of emancipation, Booker Washington came to the experience of sleeping in an ordinary bed and sitting down at table to partake of a family meal, both were a revelation of civilised existence which were quite new to him.

In a sense the very denial to the slave population of their educational rights would seem to have had something like the effect of sharpening their wits, until they became not only interested in what was happening around them, but the shrewdest observers of the signs of the times. Like other boys of his race, Booker Washington ran wild when he was not engaged in his customary errands, and without so much as learning even the English alphabet. But this compulsory ignorance seems to have intensified that ardent desire for knowledge which was part of his nature. Among his errands he might have to go to a schoolhouse where companies of happy young people were engaged over their books, and he was naturally much affected by what he saw and heard. Why was not he privileged in a similar way? Tens of thousands of negro boys may have asked themselves that same question in the generations that preceded him, and in every instance the answer would be the same — schools are forbidden to the slave. The coloured population was fast increasing, and the planters believed that the public safety could only be guaranteed by compelling them to remain illiterate.

In point of fact, however, the slaves on the plantations were not as ignorant as their too sanguine owners supposed them to be. In a secret way one here and there may even have learned to read; and, in regard to what was going on in the outside world, they were oftentimes hardly less well informed than their masters and mistresses. As Booker Washington remembers it, the time of his childhood was a wonderful era of transition. None more fully realised than the slaves themselves that the bone of contention which occasioned the Civil War was the question of slavery. Thus, to them, the period of conflict was a time of wild, but still subdued, excitement, for fear their sentiments should be detected and be followed by pains and penalties. The traffic on "the underground railroad" was probably for the time suspended; but what was called "the grapevine telegraph" was in full operation, and on every plantation and in every planter's palatial mansion the slaves looked for its messages with that ardent interest which cannot be described. They could not read newspapers, and would have been forbidden to do so had they been able, but whenever a messenger was sent to a neighbouring town he took care to linger about the post-office, or elsewhere where persons conversed on the current news, and everything that entered the coloured messenger's sharpened ears soon became generally known to every soul on the plantation. There were masters who professed to believe that their people would fight for them; but in secret nocturnal meetings these slaves congratulated one another on every Northern victory, while they prayed with pathetic ardour for the success of Lincoln and his armies.

At the same time, when they were tolerably well used by their owners, there was a good deal of sympathy binding together the coloured race and the white people. Booker Washington does not think that his race have ever betrayed any trust that has been reposed in them. Being born into slavery, they grew up without being acquainted with any other condition of life, so that it must have appeared quite natural to them for the dominant whites to live in the great house and for themselves, who were merely niggers, to herd in the cabins. But while they never undervalued freedom, and, personally, ardently longed for it, there were certain things which exercised influence over them of a softening kind, despite the master grievance of hard bondage and its occasional cruel hardships. For example, Booker Washington, at a very early age, undertook such service as he could perform in his master's house; and it was not only a possibility, it frequently happened, that a young servant, whether a lad or a girl, became a favourite with the members of the family. The younger white people would sometimes favour or protect a slave when he got into trouble, and thus something like genuine affection would be kindled in the hearts of the subject race. What animated conversations respecting the two great armies in the field such a boy as Booker Washington would hear at his master's table while he was engaged in keeping the room as clear as possible of flies! This was another way of getting the current news by those who did not form any part even of the fringe of the newspaper constituency. Then, of course, there was the constant occurrence of the usual casualties of war. Bitter sorrow and mourning, like angels of darkness, would steal into the luxurious homes of the planters when the master himself, or a son of the household, was returned invalided or so sorely wounded as to be maimed for life. It was still worse when, as it actually happened, one or another of these chief people of the Southern Confederacy was killed. There was then the anguish of mourning in the household akin to that which afflicted the people of Egypt when the first-born of each family was slain. In many cases, whether the fallen or the wounded might belong to the older or the younger generation, the slaves themselves were touched by the affliction of the family, because they never forgot the good deeds of those who had befriended them. It seems to be the belief of Booker Washington that, in any case, if, as trusted servants, they had been left in charge of a house by night or day, they would never have surrendered to the enemies of their owners, even though the invaders might have been men of the Northern battalions who were practically fighting for the freedom of the oppressed race. Still, it is thought with good reason that both the white and the coloured races were losers by slavery. As was inevitable, it turned out that one race cannot oppress another without being affected for the worse. Over the best of the plantations there seemed to hover a shadow, as though something were wanting to make the prosperity complete, when wealth was amassed by doubtful means. Instead of being a pleasure and honourable, labour was looked upon as something which had degradation associated with it. The planters and their families held aloof from it because it was the badge of slavery. The slaves themselves disliked it because it belonged to their condition of bondage.

As it has been shown, slavery reached its darkest phase in the years which immediately preceded the era of emancipation, during Booker Washington's childhood. Many telling illustrations might be given to show that this was actually the fact. I am personally well acquainted with an ex-slave, who is also a native of Virginia, who vividly remembers those days. At the time of his birth his mother was hardly more than sixteen years of age; but, notwithstanding, this girl had already tasted enough of the anguish and bitterness of slavery which might more than have sufficed for a long lifetime. She was so roughly treated by her owner that for some little time preceding her child's birth she remained concealed in a neighbouring wood, where the only diet procurable was berries or wild fruit. In this case the painful anomaly was that the slave-girl's husband was a free man who, loving his wife and child, made strenuous efforts to purchase them, but did so quite unsuccessfully. The master even moved away to another place, where the mother did the work of a domestic servant, and during this time her son experienced something of the gaiety of childhood while playing in the yard with coloured juveniles of his own age, who, like himself, were as young cattle in a pen growing up for a sad destiny.

In those days, as Booker Washington himself would be aware, slave-mothers would at times speak to their children of Georgia, or going "down South," in order to inspire terror. Going to Georgia meant to pass on into a land without hope, of darkness and death. Occasionally a hard-featured stranger would appear on the scene, and, while leaning on the fence with folded arms, he would watch the boys at play in the yard with the interested glances of a trader. Then, as must have appeared mysteriously to the boys themselves, after the stranger had gone away, one or another of the boys would be missing. Then it would be whispered, as though some horror had overtaken them, the missing boy had been taken "down South" — into Georgia.

Booker Washington is certainly one of the most extraordinary examples on record of the successful pursuit of knowledge under difficulties; but there have been many striking examples among slaves of lads showing this mettle. My ex-slave friend, to whom reference has been made, is certainly to be reckoned as one of these. It is probable that his mother may have passed as a woman of education, seeing that she knew the English alphabet and was able to count a hundred. Be this as it may, however, like a genuine Christian mother, she determined that, in spite of planters and their laws, her child should learn whatever she could teach him. In due course the boy himself showed a flaming desire to learn. By dint of remarkable diligence and perseverance, he got ahead of his mother in knowledge. If learning was carried on in secret, there had rarely been found a more ardent pupil. Without inconvenient questions being asked, he succeeded in purchasing a copy-book and spelling primer, which were well used on all possible occasions. He actually went through the whole of the Bible when he could not master more than one in eight of the words. This man afterwards enjoyed the benefit of a college education in England, so that his case is worthy of being mentioned as being similar to that of Booker Washington. Both instances alike show that negroes may not only have good intellectual endowments, but may also succeed in high aims by dint of unflagging energy and perseverance.

At length the era of freedom came; and although at that time Booker Washington was still too young to realise what all the excitement and commotion portended, those who looked upon him saw the child who would develop into a benefactor of his race and the most distinguished negro of his time. The Man who was wanted was found.

CHAPTER II

THE ERA OF FREEDOM — REALISIN\G THAT KNOWLEDGE IS POWER

The great, long-looked-for and ardently-prayed-for day of freedom had come at last, and probably one of the things which Booker Washington remembers is the kiss which his mother gave him after listening to the reading of President Lincoln's Proclamation, and to which the Southern leaders were compelled to yield when the pressure of the Northern army became too great to be longer resisted. In common justice to the Southern planters, we have to remember that the crisis may have meant little if anything short of actual ruin. The human chattels, as slaves were often called, were not seldom very valuable bargains in the open market. A sum of 3000 dollars in gold was once offered for the ex-slave friend to whom reference has been made, and was at once refused by his owner. It can well be believed that one who has developed such a gift for organisation as Booker Washington would have commanded a much higher figure, although such prices were, of course, far in advance of the average.

It might also be said that the planters were not responsible for slavery having become an institution of the Republic, and that they had to do with things as they found them. But while this may be true, it has also to be admitted that the Southern States retained that institution longer than their neighbours. At the end of the century in which the Republic secured its independence there were under 900,000 slaves in the whole of the United States; but the total was nearly 4,000,000 in the year of emancipation. The Northern States had already liberated their slaves in a gradual way about a quarter of a century before that crisis. For generations slavery had been denounced as a wrong, amounting to a great evil, by a number of chief men among the Republican leaders, such as Franklin and Washington, Madison and Jefferson, and others. These men were sufficiently outspoken to regard the thing as being quite out of keeping with the principles of the Declaration of Independence. Nevertheless, differences of opinion over this matter not only led to violent controversy but to religious division, the most notable split being that of the Episcopal Methodist Church, which henceforth had its Northern and Southern sections, the latter being founded on a pro-slavery basis.

Young as he was when the great revolution of complete abolition in the Southern States was brought about, Booker Washington was still able to show a child's keenest interest in what was taking place. It was as if the sun had risen on new times altogether; the very winds seemed to blow more cheerfully; the sky above seemed to be bright with promise with better things to come than mere *niggers* had ever known before; it was as though the Golden Age itself had dawned. The sharp-witted little son of the slave-girl could heartily enter into his mother's joy, but he could not take in the meaning of the things that were happening as he has been able to understand them since. Such a child was naturally affected by the growing boldness and enthusiasm of his elders, who for some time before the final catastrophe clearly anticipated what the end would be. When they gathered at their nocturnal meetings there was unwonted light in their eyes; a spirit of hope and cheerfulness such as they had never known before gave new life to their hymns, which had too often been sad or weird; their feelings became irrepressible. There were signs and tokens of various kinds which the working slaves well understood, whatever this child of a slave-mother may have made of them. There was something in the air which told that something uncommon was coming — "a sound of going in the tops of the mulberry trees," as it were, which betokened that the great day of freedom had come. Straggling soldiers, who had broken away from the Confederate Army, had a doleful story to tell of disaster and collapse. Then, besides, the inmates of the great house were thinking of how best they could secure their valuables if the invaders actually came. Then, on the first Sunday of April 1865, the catastrophe may be said to have really come. On that day vast quantities of stores were burned at Richmond; during the night many a slave-owner stole away, and in the early morning numbers who had been slaves found themselves no longer in bondage when they greeted the regiments of the Northern Army.

Booker Washington testifies to the wild excess of joy with which the slaves on all the plantations accepted the freedom which had come to them in this remarkable, but no doubt providential, way. For the moment they took no account of the future; they were altogether intoxicated while trying to estimate the reality of that new condition in which they found themselves — that inestimable blessing about which their forefathers had prayed through long and weary generations. The thing seemed to be too good to be true, and yet it was actually with them — it was their own blissful possession!

Then, as was inevitable, human nature being what it is, there came a somewhat strong reaction to this outburst of feeling and irrepressible excitement. What about the future? Practically, a whole nation of something like 4,000,000 persons had suddenly been set free, severed from their employment and their masters, who in their way had looked after them. Those masters had been sorely reduced by the war; many members of the great houses had been killed or wounded. What was to become of those millions of coloured people who had never come in contact with the outer world, who, with a few exceptions, were quite illiterate and knew nothing of the outside world? No wonder that a certain amount of gloom and misgiving soon took the place of that exuberance of joy which the sense of freedom had at first inspired. The crisis was sufficiently serious for those who were young and strong, but what was to become of the aged or those who were worn out in the hard service of the plantations?

Probably the gloom which now overtook so many of the coloured people was as exaggerated as their wild ideas about their good fortune when freedom first came to them. These coloured folk were apt to run into extremes. Booker Washington well remembers them in both moods; and he also can call to mind how they came to see that, after all, liberty was an inheritance of sterling worth when it was fairly estimated. One advantage of the new-found freedom consisted in possessing the right to choose a respectable surname; and another gain was the right, if they felt so disposed, to leave the old haunts and, in some measure, to look round the outside world. Otherwise, they could hardly tell how it might feel to be free. As is the case with agricultural labourers in general, these poor coloured slave folk, with whom Booker Washington was acquainted, had never been far afield from the place of their birth, and, having seen so little of the world, they found that the world was a wide place and, in some respects, different from what they had expected. Of course, a large number were glad to return to the plantations and to agree with their old employers to work as labourers. In choosing their new names, the ex-slaves showed some good taste as well as ambition. Having the patronymic list of presidents, statesmen, soldiers and others to select from, they bedecked themselves in becoming style, not forgetting a middle and, apparently, an initial letter, which usually did not represent a name at all, but, as showing the American manner, was still indispensable. Even in the case of the distinguished negro, an account of whose life and work is given in this volume, he had no such name as Booker T. Washington while he remained in a state of slavery; he chose it for himself after he became free, and all must admit that he made a good selection.

Mrs Washington — as by courtesy she may be called — did not return to the fields after gaining her freedom, as was the case with so many of her old companions. Circumstances led to her removal to Malden, in West Virginia, and which is also in the suburbs of Charleston. Still being quite a young lad, Booker Washington accompanied his mother, as did also his brother John, the object being to join their mother's husband — the man being only their stepfather — who was then employed in the salt industry.

Notwithstanding that all were now free, the temporal prosperity of the family so far showed no improvement. Amid the huts and furnaces of the salt-producing little town there was even less comfort, and far more repulsive squalor, than there had been on the plantation among fellow-slaves. Being a mixture of coloured and white people, the main part were a degraded set; so that, after all the toil and rough adventure of some weeks of travelling, the wonder is that the future benefactor of his race was not utterly demoralised amid his new surroundings. Perhaps it turned out to his advantage that he had to work hard through very long days.

Ever since the time that he began to think about anything, Booker Washington had been inspired by a very strong desire to learn to read. He resolved that, come what might, he would, if possible, so far distinguish himself as to become competent to read the periodicals and newspapers of the day. This was a very praiseworthy resolution to make, but to ordinary persons how utterly impossible of attainment it must have seemed when all things were against them. By a roundabout way he so far advanced as to be able to understand what certain figures on a salt-barrel meant; but he had not even a primer or spelling-book until, on being earnestly requested to do so, his mother was successful in her strenuous endeavours to obtain one. In the whole circle of his coloured acquaintance the ex-slave child knew of no individual who could read, his mother being no exception. This fact, however, seems to have the effect of bringing out in bolder outline the sterling traits of this negro woman's character. She was evidently uncommonly shrewd in worldly matters, and, instead of advising her child not to attempt what might well have seemed to be impossibilities, she showed that wholesome ambition for the boy's future which proved her to be of a superior nature, while she was a genuine, loving mother. We may be sure that Booker Washington inherited his gifts and indomitable perseverance from his mother. A long line of distinguished men have borne similar testimony. Men who have lived and laboured for the benefit of others have been, in very many instances, what their mothers made them.

Having obtained his spelling-book, Booker Washington commenced his education without a teacher, the consequence being that he was occupied for some weeks in overcoming the difficulties of the alphabet, which, under the most favourable conditions, would have detained him but a few hours. In due course he made more rapid progress under the teaching of a negro boy who had the rare distinction of being able to read a printed page; and, as was quite natural, such an example of literary attainments in youth was no less envied than admired.

Then something else occurred which cannot fail to strike us as being almost a phenomenon — at all events, a thing altogether extraordinary under the circumstances. What, through the vista of a third of a century, looks like a perfect *furore* for education took complete possession of the ex-slaves, and, what made this the more singular, the burning desire for school teaching extended to aspirants of all ages. Before philanthropists came forward to help them the coloured people were found to have their own appointed tutor, and care was taken that he should fare well. Thus, in the case of Booker Washington, the first comparatively competent teacher with whom he came in contact was a quondam soldier who had served in the war. Surely no tutor ever had more enthusiastic pupils; and whether the age of the learner was seven or seventy-five, it seemed to make no difference in damping their enthusiasm. Indeed, it may be seriously questioned whether any other race of people would ever have rivalled this extraordinary ardour in learning to read. And circumstances made it necessary that even the Sunday schools, in common with the day schools, should, first of all, give the most elementary of teaching. What a contrast such a state of things presents to anything of the kind with which we are familiar in connection with any other country! How many there are who remain illiterate, or semi-illiterate, in spite of the schools which are provided and admirably equipped under any national system of education! In their darkest days of ignorance and bondage the negro slaves showed the most lively desire for education. In what measure is that true of any other race? We know that through a long succession of centuries our own peasantry remained, for the most part, quite illiterate, all the while showing a kind of sullen content or stolid indifference. That negroes should show other characteristics should inspire the encouragement coming from the hope that they are destined for better things than have usually entered into the calculations of American politicians. It is because Booker Washington so thoroughly well understands his race that he can harbour such bright hopes of their future, provided that common-sense means are used to train and educate them, so as to give them an opportunity of making the best possible use of their capacities. He is quite an ingenuous man, who says just what he thinks, and who would never think of aiming at the impracticable. What may at first have seemed to be quite a Utopian enterprise to quidnuncs in

American social and political circles is to him a very ordinary business. He has solved what has been to others a dark problem, because he has failed to see that there was any problem which needed solution. He sees in the labour of the millions of negroes who people the Southern States a source of vast national wealth. Only turn this to good account and the whole country will be benefited and enriched, while the descendants of the ex-slaves themselves will remain contented and good citizens. To carry out this idea is certainly one of the greatest of enterprises to which social reformers in the New World have ever set their hand.

When a school was established and a supposed competent tutor was appointed, Booker Washington did not find that his course had ceased to be a pursuit of knowledge under difficulties. His mother and stepmother were so poor that it was not thought that his services at the salt works could be altogether dispensed with in order that he might attend school. Then a kind of compromise was made, and without the work being entirely suspended, he was allowed to pass some portion of each day at the school. Having thus risen to this respectable standing, he found it desirable to wear a cap which his mother made for him; for it would seem that a Virginian planter no more thought of providing such head-dress for boy slaves than he would of clothing his colts or calves. It was then, moreover, that he gave himself the name which he has ever since retained and honoured. He had been called Booker as a child-slave; for some reason his mother had added Taliaferro, but the final Washington was a becoming euphonism of his own.

With so much manual labour to be done, the difficulties in the way of education were continually becoming intensified. Soon it became impossible to continue in attendance at the day school, and he had to be content with attending an evening class after completing the day's toil. Under the most favourable circumstances this was exhausting; and his experience proved still more trying when he was removed from the salt works to serve in a coal mine, which supplied the furnaces with fuel. Booker Washington has very vivid recollections of the horrors and even constant dangers attending such subterranean work. The darkness alone was almost such as might be felt; and the mishaps, through taking a wrong path, through falling coal, or a candle getting extinguished, were ever threatening those engaged in the works. It was in such an atmosphere and amid such surroundings, however, that the dawn of a new era sent its beams across his chequered pathway. It was there that he heard for the first time of the Hampton Normal and Agricultural Institute, which was destined to shape for him his life-course. The institution in question is near to the small town and bathing resort of Hampton, in Virginia, and the channel, commanded by Fortress Monroe, was the scene of some lively naval fights during the Civil War. The institution was founded in 1868 by General S. C. Armstrong, and two years later was incorporated by the State of Virginia. Its object is stated to be "to train young men and women of the negro and Indian races to become teachers among their own people." Booker Washington happened to overhear two men in the coal mine conversing together about this school, and he resolved to find out everything possible about it. The revelation had for him something more than passing interest; strange new hopes had been kindled in his soul. If he had asked, Who was Samuel Chapman Armstrong? he might have learned that he was an officer who had served in the Civil War, and that he was born in the Hawaiian Islands in 1839. The General was a genuine, warm-hearted friend of the coloured races, and as he became to Booker Washington an exemplar, or even something like an apostle, who did more than any other human teacher to mark out his pathway of life, some reference may be made to the pressing needs of the freed negroes in the years which immediately followed the close of the Civil War. There are now some ten million coloured people in the Southern States, but at the time in question there were less than half of this number. Nevertheless, the crisis was sufficiently serious to be even alarming. Thus a contemporary writer says: —

"Such sudden emancipation, on so vast a scale, is unequalled in the annals of history. The nearest parallel to it is the deliverance of the Israelites from Egyptian bondage. A nation, numbering about two millions, was then suddenly emancipated. But as for their sustenance and preservation a succession of miracles took place, it is not necessary for our present purpose to pursue the parallel. No instance in secular history equals the present position of the freed negroes of North America. The crisis has come in a manner and at a time that could hardly have been anticipated by the wisest forecaster of political events."

Great as was the need for earnest effort after hostilities ceased, however, the want and suffering had been far more acute in days that had gone before. The contemporary writer just quoted adds: —

"From the very beginning of the war hundreds have suddenly poured in, as at an hour's notice, upon the cities of the Northern States. One of the camps was inundated by a thousand of these naked and starving fugitives in a single day, and this whilst the snow was coldly and silently covering the surrounding landscape. After the Federals had gained possession of Memphis, there speedily turned into it a long train of negroes, so miserably destitute that, having nothing whatever with them of food or clothing but the rags of two or three years' wear, and only the clouds and the trees to shelter them, these human multitudes were far worse off than the comfortably-kennelled dogs of their white brethren. When General Sherman passed through Georgia, he was asked how many negroes had followed his army. The reply was, 'Ten miles of them.'"

Charitable and Christian people were moved to do what lay in their power not only to relieve present sufferings, but to enable the coloured folk to make a new start in the world. Associations were formed, money was collected, even the Government took care that rations should be distributed. The result was that the outlook soon showed signs of improvement. At one time Levi Coffin of Cincinnati reported that there were thirty-five camps in the Mississippi Valley which contained about 650,000 coloured fugitives, but these camps soon became self-supporting. The more acute want and suffering were soon relieved, but it soon became more and more apparent that service of a more permanent kind would have to be undertaken if the coloured people were to be raised from the low condition into which slavery had reduced them. People of the shrewder sort clearly saw that great results might be expected from education and industrial training. Although the prevailing ignorance was of the densest kind, all were most anxious to learn. Wherever a camp appeared it was certain that schools would speedily follow; and in what must have appeared an incredibly short space of time no less than 250 schools were established in that Mississippi Valley alone. The contemporary anonymous writer in the *Leisure Hour* who has already been quoted, and who appears to have been thoroughly well acquainted with the negroes' characteristics and condition in their transition state, adds this word-picture of the general outlook at the time to which reference is being made: —

"They are most anxious to be taught, and most docile under direction. Their ignorance previously was universal and extreme. It is no wonder that their religious camp-meetings had become associated with the most grotesque ideas and narrations. It is no wonder that their phraseology was a caricature of civilised language. For how could they be expected to manifest intelligence without any education? So deplorably destitute of instruction were they that very few even of their preachers could read the simplest words. Old men amongst them who had preached the Gospel to their black congregations for upwards of forty years, were found totally ignorant of the alphabet, and, of course, had never read a verse of Scripture. How could the Sermons, the prayers and the religious ideas of such 'pastors' be other than grievously deficient?"

When the depressed conditions under which these coloured people had previously lived were duly taken into account, the most wonderful thing of all was seen in the rapid strides they made in the betterment of their temporal condition or outward surroundings. The days no longer passed in dull or even painful monotony. Labour, which had hitherto been to them hard bondage, not easy to bear, had become a privilege and a pleasure. Having survived the too exaggerated notions of what the new era might mean for them, and the inevitable reaction of disappointment which followed, they could now take stock of life and realise that they had been enormous gainers by at last coming into that inheritance for which their forefathers had so earnestly longed and prayed. The responsibilities, and even the commonplace things associated with freedom, were intensely prized. In contrast with the loose and demoralising customs which had been characteristic of slave-worked plantations, marriage became a bond not to be dissolved. Now that they were becoming able to read it for themselves, the Bible became a prized book, which the negroes regarded as being peculiarly their own. So far from disappointing those who sought to aid them, now that their ex-owners, the planters, were so greatly impoverished, or even ruined, the negroes surprised their friends by the readiness with which they adapted themselves to their new life. The way in which habits of industry and economy were formed struck observers with peculiar force, as being an exceedingly hopeful sign. Nor did the freer air, which they now breathed, in any measure weaken those Christian ties which had held them together in their days of bondage. Their religious meetings were well maintained, but of course under happier conditions. The sad or even strangely weird songs which had been sung by night with bated breath, as it were, in the slave-cabins could now be superseded by more cheerful hymns. The former had been the natural expression of bond-slaves, to whom life on earth was without hope; at last they were able to sing the triumphant note of freemen. He was a very representative member of the negro race who at that time remarked to a friend, "I'se afeard I'll work myself to death now. I'se so glad to work for myself and the family that I can't stop nohow." Even in the United States, where towns and large communities have often risen rapidly in what had but just before been the wilderness, this new reformation, which the negroes now proved themselves to be capable of keeping pace with, must have struck many observers as a phenomenon for which they had hardly been prepared. Schoolhouses and churches, as well as cottages, which were a grateful contrast to the squalid cabins of the plantations, were in many instances supplemented by savings banks. At the same time a disposition towards self-reliance showed itself, which led the main body, whenever possible, to keep aloof from the alms-houses, in which pauper poor were sheltered, by working hard and bravely to support themselves and their households.

While this transition age was in progress, Booker Washington was growing up apace. He had been fortunate enough to sever his connection with the Malden salt-furnaces and their squalid and immoral surroundings, and, what was still better, he had escaped from the coal mine never to return, and had found more genial employment in the household of a military officer and his wife. He now worked more ardently than ever towards the Hampton Institute.

CHAPTER III

OFF TO HAMPTON —
WAS HE A LIKELY CANDIDATE?

Those who read the American newspapers will be aware that there is great diversity of opinion in regard to the manner in which the education of the coloured people should be conducted. Those who have grown up amid the traditions of the Southern States, where, under the old order of things, the education of slaves was a legal offence, do not readily favour that higher training of negroes to which, in Great Britain, no one would ever think of offering any objection. The feeling referred to prevails in the Northern States as well as in the Southern; and more or less throughout the Republic it is strongly held that, whether educated or uneducated, the coloured race are socially on a lower plane and can never associate on terms of equality with white people. The readiness with which he has acknowledged this fact, while acting accordingly, has in no small measure contributed to Booker Washington's success and popularity. He has undoubtedly stimulated the interest which is now shown in efficient negro training, as is self-evident from the newspaper and magazine articles which from time to time appear upon the subject. Thus, in course of an article on "The Function of the Negro College," in the *Dial* of Chicago, Mr Kelly Miller, of Howard University, Washington, remarks: —

"The groundwork of education cannot be modified to meet the variant demands of race or colour, previous conditions or present needs. The general processes of discipline and culture must form a fixed and unalterable part of any adequate educational programme. On the other hand, there is quite a wide latitude of accommodation for special needs and social circumstances in what might be called the practical aspect of education. There has recently sprung up a class of educational philosophers who would restrict the term practical education to those forms of knowledge or formulas of information which can be converted into cash equivalent on demand. The truth is, that all knowledge which enables the recipient to do with added efficiency the work which falls to his lot in this world, whether that work be tilling the soil or plying a handicraft, healing the sick or enlightening the ignorant, uplifting the lowly or administering spiritual solace, is 'practical' in the highest and best significance of that term. . . . Traditional branches of study have lost much of their talismanic value. The so-called higher education is no longer confined to the classic tongues of two famous far-off peoples. The pedagogical watchword is *method* rather than subject-matter. The higher method of inquiry and investigation can be applied to the growing roots of living plants as well as to the dry stems of a dead language. The problems growing out of the population of Alabama or Florida are as intricate in their relation, and as far-reaching in their consequence, and, withal, as important a subject for study, as any ever involved in the European peninsulas."

It seems to be generally held by such writers and their readers that the mission of negroes who have received a good college training is to be teachers and leaders to the more commonplace members of their own race, and it is thought that a proportion of one in two hundred needs to have the knowledge which will enable him to lead, and so benefit his fellows. There must be tact, however; the negro student must have his craft well ballasted or he may lose self-control, which may possibly lead to somewhat comical results. Thus, Mr Miller tells of "A circular issued by a young man, scarcely thirty years of age, the sum-total of whose knowledge would be scarcely equal to that of a Yale sophomore, who advertises himself as Rev. — — , A.M., B.D., Ph.D., D.D. It is more than likely that the majority of the congregation of this over-bedecked preacher can neither read nor write. What these humble people need is sound knowledge and simple sense. . . . The negro race is characterised by boisterousness of manners and extravagant forms of taste. As if to correct such deficiencies, their higher education hitherto has been largely concerned with Greek and Latin literature, the norms of modern culture. The advanced negro student became acquainted with Homer and Virgil before he had Shakespeare and Milton. It is just here that our educational critics are apt to become excited. The spectacle of a negro wearing eyeglasses, and declaiming in classic phrases about 'the walls of lofty Rome,' and 'the wrath of Achilles,' upsets their critical balance and composure. We have so often listened to the grotesque incongruity of a Greek chorus and a greasy cabin, and the relative value of a piano and a patch of potatoes, that if we did not join in the smile in order to encourage the humour, we should do so out of sheer weariness."

Their utterances show in what light the college training of negroes is regarded by ordinary citizens of the United States; and it may be noted that Mr Kelly Miller, the writer, hails from Howard University, which is intended chiefly for coloured students. As slavery only disappeared a generation ago, it can hardly be expected that such a matter can be discussed without some show of extravagance or of exaggeration appearing. We even find a well-known Doctor of Divinity venturing the opinion, in an influential weekly journal, that the education of one white student is worth more to the negroes than the education of ten blacks. All tends to clear the air, however; and what is done at Howard and Atlanta Universities and elsewhere, in the way of providing education for coloured youths, shows that advances are being made, and that better times are coming.

We left Booker Washington still looking forward with confidence to being admitted as a student at Hampton College and Industrial Institute. The resolution thus taken was the more extraordinary because the negro aspirant was still a mere boy, practically without means for such an ambitious enterprise, while he had no friends who could assist him in any adequate manner. He was also quite unused to travelling, and was so unacquainted with the map of his native State that he could not have pointed out the direction in which the town of Hampton lay. In point of fact, a cross-country journey would have to be taken, representing a distance about corresponding with that between London and Aberdeen. Under such unfavourable conditions even his hitherto heroic mother, whose strength seemed now to be declining, hardly thought that the thing could successfully be carried out. On the other hand, others rather encouraged the lad, at least to make the endeavour. Then, for some considerable time before the start was made, the outlook at Malden, so far as Booker Washington was himself personally concerned, had considerably improved. Instead of having to continue at the rough, or even dangerous, labour in which he had been compelled to engage, he obtained a situation in the household of a military officer, whose wife had gained the reputation of being a domestic martinet, the family otherwise being one of the chief in the town. The sequel proved, however, that common report is oftentimes not to be trusted; for while the ex-slave boy made an excellent house-servant, the discipline he underwent in the officer's house was just such as he needed, and could not fail to be beneficial to him.

Having resolved to resign a situation which he valued, and which, most probably, his mother would have been well content for him to retain, the would-be student prepared to start, being unhampered by anything in the way of luggage beyond a bundle that could easily be carried in one hand. The journey alone was a very formidable undertaking, much more so at that time than would be the case today. As might have been expected, the ambitious youth soon made the painful discovery that he was very inadequately equipped for his journey. The difficulties of the way were also greatly increased by the fact that he belonged to a proscribed race. The distance was so great that money was wanted for food and for travelling fares; but the scant available supply very speedily ran out. Of course, there were roadside houses of rest and of refreshment into which negroes could not gain admittance, even though he might carry a good supply of cash. He soon found out that a boy of colour could not hope to find lodging in an hotel intended for white people; and on reaching Richmond, footsore and famished with hunger, he was so utterly impecunious that, for some nights in succession, after earning a little by day, he had to repeat the experience of "sleeping out." The wonder is that, in the case of so young a boy, all of this suffering did not damp his ardour and discourage his still persevering. So far as can be discovered, however, he never did lose his hold of the anchor of hope. Is it not a singular and a suggestive thing that quite a number of well-known men, who afterwards won literary fame or distinguished commercial success, were correspondingly adventurous in having to "sleep out," or to walk the streets through the livelong night in order to keep themselves warm, because they lacked the money wherewith to pay for a bed? Dr Johnson went through this experience before he became the literary autocrat of the eighteenth century. So also did John Cassell when he came to London, with only a few pence in his pocket, not so very long before the founding of that printing and publishing house, still named after him, which ranks as one of the greatest establishments of the kind in the British Isles.

No youthful aspirant thirsting for an education ever completed a more toilsome, and even painful, journey in order to reach the college he desired to enter than Booker Washington, when he actually got over the five hundred miles between Malden and Hampton. It is still more remarkable that, although he was undoubtedly one of the most daring and doggedly persevering youths that could have been found among the coloured people, he was still not a solitary example of a negro boy literally making stepping-stones of difficulties. There were other black youngsters who were quite as determined, and their efforts were also destined to be crowned with success.

Still, our wonder is increased when we remember that this journey, with its formidable difficulties, was boldly hazarded without there being any certainty of his being received as a student in the institution. No one in the house even knew that he was on the road and was about to present himself as a candidate for admission.

When at length he arrived and confronted the chief matron, a less shrewd and sympathetic person than she was would hardly have been impressed in Booker Washington's favour. Footsore, travel-stained, hungry, with not more than two shillings in his pocket, he was, in point of fact, so completely, though unintentionally, disguised, that an ordinary observer would have had difficulty in deciding what he was. He might have been one of that class, who abound in the United States, who prefer a wandering vagabond life to honest work, and who thus thought that a brief acquaintance with the college might add to the diversity or excitement of life. But, happily, there is something in the human eye which surely betokens character. Cheats and impostors of all kinds cannot control their eyes. It would seem that the chief matron thought that there might be something in the adventurous applicant. At all events she decided that he might be tested, and, as the training included the teaching of various industries, what more effective test could be applied than the "doing up" of a room. The work was so perfectly done that Booker Washington was found to have something in him.

We may naturally infer that this aspiring negro lad now began fully to reap the benefit of having been for many months subjected to the uncompromising discipline of the domestic martinet — the general's wife — at Malden. If it had not been for this preliminary household education we can hardly suppose that he would, even imperfectly, have understood how to do certain things which were now done well, the knowledge thus acquired being of the greatest possible value to one who had to make a favourable impression on those from whom he was hoping to obtain an education. He was admitted into the institution as a student; but as there were still certain expenses for board and teaching to be met, difficulties looming in the future were not as yet altogether overcome. It was quite impossible for him to find any money at all for current expenses unless it was first earned, all of his family connections being too poor to send even the smallest contribution. The most ready way out of such difficulties was for the student to give his labour during certain hours of each day in return for his board. He was such an efficient house-servant that such an arrangement promised to be of advantage to both sides. He was appointed to the position of what we should call handy-man in the institution — doorkeeper, porter, room-cleaner, man-of-all-work. The burden of labour, in addition to onerous class-work, which all this involved through each successively long working day, was, of course, formidable; but such things were now made light of because the goal, so long looked forward to when seen from afar, had been reached at last. The ex-slave boy not only breathed the air of freedom, he was getting an education which was best adapted to his needs and future plans. General Armstrong, the founder of such a school-paradise, was naturally looked upon as an ideal man. Until the good General died in middle age, Booker Washington never lowered his estimate of this distinguished benefactor of the coloured race; and, if questioned at the present time concerning his late friend, the master of the Tuskegee institution would probably not hesitate to say that the General was worthy of being compared with Greatheart in the *Pilgrim's Progress*.

During those early days at Hampton there were, at times, hardships to be borne, but even these seem to have had a bracing effect. The number of students became so great that those who had to be lodged in tents might occasionally suffer from the weather. Notwithstanding, coloured students made light of privations which might reasonably have damped the ardour of others.

CHAPTER IV

GENERAL ARMSTRONG —
HIS PREDECESSORS AND COLLABORATORS —
PIONEERS OF THE NEW ERA

When in 1868, some years after the close of the Civil War, General Armstrong proceeded to give practical expression to his idea of founding a normal and industrial institute for the coloured races, which are found within the boundaries of the great American Republic, the new era of education for such peoples, which had been made possible by the emancipation of the slaves in the Southern States, was fast coming on. Of course, General Armstrong was not the original pioneer in such service; but it may probably come to pass that he will be the best remembered on account of his having trained such a distinguished pupil as Booker Washington. But for years prior to his making the acquaintance of this Virginian boy, the work carried on by the General must have won for him some considerable amount of popularity; otherwise, what was being done would hardly have become a matter of conversation between miners in a coal-mine. Had that talk not taken place, the institution at Tuskegee might possibly not have been quite what it is today.

What has been effected, and what is still being done, is seen to be all very wonderful when it is compared with the state of things, as well as the kind of popular sentiment which formerly existed, not only in the South, but even in the Northern States. There was a time when public prejudice made it impossible, or almost impossible, to educate coloured pupils at all whether they were free or otherwise. Such far-reaching institutions as General Armstrong founded at Hampton, and, still more notably, the one which his pupil and disciple has planted and built up with a masterly hand at Tuskegee, are nothing less than signs of the times, which indicate to the American people, and to the world, that a mighty revolution has taken place, and is still working out its beneficent purposes.

Some time ago an article in *Scribner's Magazine* revived the memories which cluster around the name of Prudence Crandall, of Windham County, Connecticut. Who was this woman? In a volume of autobiographical recollections and reminiscences published in 1887, Laura S. Haviland thus answers this question: —

> "She opened a school in Canterbury Green for girls, and was patronised by the best families, not only of that town, but of other counties and states. Among those who

sought advantages of her school was a coloured girl. But Prudence was too thorough a Quaker to regard the request of bitter prejudice on the part of her other patrons to dismiss her coloured pupil. But she did not wait for them to execute their threat to withdraw their children. She sent them home. Then she advertised her school as a boarding-school for young ladies of colour. The people felt insulted, and held indignation meetings and appointed committees to remonstrate with her. But she stood to her principles regardless of their remonstrance. The excitement in that town ran high. A town meeting was called to devise means to remove the nuisance. . . . Miss Crandall opened her school against the protest of an indignant populace. Another town meeting was called at which it was resolved, 'That the establishment of a rendezvous, falsely denominated a school, was designed by its projectors as the theatre to promulgate their disgusting theory of amalgamation, and their pernicious sentiments of subverting the Union. These pupils were to have been congregated here from all quarters under the false pretence of educating them, but really to scatter firebrands, arrows and death among brethren of our own blood.'"

In the darkest days the above would appear to reflect the popular sentiment in regard to negro education even in the Northern States, although there were still thousands of persons to be found who had no manner of sympathy with such views. Neither the teacher nor her coloured pupils were allowed to attend the ordinary religious service at the Congregational Church; her parents were forbidden to visit Miss Crandall; she was threatened with arrest as a criminal; her windows and doors were destroyed with crowbars, and the house was set on fire. The school had to be given up; but the example of the heroic teacher had not been in vain. As Laura Haviland remarks, "her name became a household word in thousands of Northern homes." A similar revolution for the better will surely be brought about in the Southern States also, and is even now in progress. We can hardly doubt that after some further progress has been made there will be nothing within their power that the good old families of the South will not do for the negroes when they find that the coloured race is amenable to civilising influences, and that commercially they will well repay for all the money and trouble that may be expended upon them. At the outset of this reformation this must have been the hope of General Armstrong; and it would seem to be that of Booker Washington at Tuskegee today.

In some instances the pioneer teachers had to carry on their service amid the lowest depths of squalor and wretchedness, even more repellent than ragged-school work in the worst quarters of a great town. Thus, Mrs Haviland, in her autobiography, tells how Dr Emily P. Newcomb, who was said to come of a family of educators, bravely founded a station at Kansas City, and herself superintended the work: —

"At this point there is massed a large population of exceedingly ignorant, destitute and superstitious people of every colour and condition — men, women and children — crowded together in rickety hovels, where stagnant water stood the year round, the very air impregnated with the heavy sickening odour of the packing-houses. No tongue or pen can describe the wretchedness that existed in that locality, known and appropriately designated as Hell's Half Acre, which embraced a large area on either side of the State line. At that time no mission work had been attempted or suggested for the elevation of this seething mass by either Church or State."

For bravery in her work and devotion, we find Emily Newcomb, M.D., compared to a general on the battlefield. From such a woman's working experience, as well as from that of others who were like-minded, we can in some measure estimate the magnitude of the work which required to be done. The suddenness of their emancipation, and the consequent disorganisation of their social life, could not but involve a good deal of suffering. In regard to the general condition of the coloured people at the time in question, Mr F. J. Loudin says: "They were homeless, penniless, ignorant, improvident — unprepared in every way for the dangers as well as the duties of freedom. Self-reliance they had never had the opportunity to learn, and, suddenly left to shift for themselves, they were at the mercy of the knaves who were everywhere so ready to cheat them out of their honest earnings." They were a people who were too often despised on the one hand, and yet as often showing extraordinary traits of character on the other. There were gems of the first water among them; and now and then an individual, showing in one person the best attributes of both races, came to the front. It became more and more evident that the chief kind of aid which these people wanted was being taught how to help themselves. One of the mettle of Booker Washington could push his way upward, braving and overcoming obstacles and difficulties such as might well have cowed a youth who possessed the courage and perseverance of a dozen men; but he was one of a thousand, one who was destined to become a pioneer who would make the way plainer and easier for those who followed after. However low down they might be, the coloured race showed no disposition to remain where they were; all along the line were seen signs of advancement. As regarded the proportion who attended religious worship, and who were Church communicants, the negroes compared favourably with the whites. Persons who carefully took notice of the different phases of the new reformation in progress were often having some new surprise. Thus, the manner in which the funds were raised for the building and endowment of Fisk University seems almost to belong to the region of romance, as is proved from this opening passage in the popular volume which contains the narrative: —

"The story of the Jubilee Singers seems almost as little like a chapter from real life as the legend of the daring Argonauts who sailed with Jason on that famous voyage after the Golden Fleece. It is the story of a little company of emancipated slaves who set out to secure, by their singing, the fabulous sum of twenty thousand dollars for the impoverished and unknown school in which they were students. The world was as unfamiliar to these untravelled free people as were the countries through which the Argonauts had to pass; the social prejudices that confronted them were as terrible to meet as fire-breathing bulls or the warriors that sprang from the land sown with dragons' teeth; and no seas were ever more tempestuous than the stormy experiences that for a time tested their faith and courage. They were at times without the money to buy needed clothing. Yet in less than three years they returned, bringing back with them nearly one hundred thousand dollars. They had been turned away from hotels and driven out of railway waiting-rooms because of their colour. But they had been received with honour by the President of the United States; they had sung their slave-songs before the Queen of Great Britain, and they had gathered, as invited guests, about the breakfast-table of her Prime Minister. Their success was as remarkable as their mission was unique."

The University for coloured students, on behalf of which these efforts were made, is situated at Nashville, a town which, on account of the number and quality of its educational institutions, has come to be called the Athens of the South. Its first students consisted of those who had actually been slaves; and the earnestness of most of the students had to bear the test of having to earn their own livelihood while receiving their education. Outside aid was given in the hope that an endowment would be provided. The college, including its Jubilee Hall and Livingstone Hall, occupies a healthy site, and has grounds of twenty-five acres. The negroes are in a minority at Nashville; but it is there that one may profitably study their characteristic traits and capacities, and thus form some tolerably correct estimate of what the vast national gain would be if the entire coloured race were raised by adequate education and industrial training.

In aiming at what he does in founding and carrying on his great institution at Tuskegee, is Booker Washington warranted by the past successes of those who have worked to raise and train negroes for the best service of which they are capable, in harbouring the sanguine anticipations he does for more perfect achievements in the future? As he is happily only one, though the chief, worker among many, it will be necessary, while proceeding with our story, to give convincing testimony from outsiders concerning the reasonableness and practicableness of his aims and hopes. In giving some interesting and striking illustrations by way of proof that he is no visionary, but a cool-headed, hard-working calculator who well knows that the capital he is working with will yield a high percentage, we may have to tell of what is in progress in Nashville itself.

CHAPTER V

UPS AND DOWNS — PROGRESS AS A
STUDENT — BEGINNING TO TEACH

Probably one reason why youths who are educated in such a school as the Hampton Normal and Agricultural Institute so commonly turn out to be of use to themselves and to others in the world is, that only young people of mettle and perseverance would endure the labour and hardship which form part of the discipline. What was done for the students was not altogether gratuitous; they were supposed either to have means or to be able to earn money, and to be too hard driven to be able to pay the merest trifle may often have been an experience which might have damped the ardour of any save enthusiasts of the most dogged perseverance. Among the large company of poor students, it would almost seem that Booker Washington was the poorest. Do what he would, he could not help small arrears of college dues accumulating; and when vacation time came round, he might be the only one of the household who could not afford to rejoin his friends at home. Instead of thinking of doing this, there was pressing necessity for finding work in the town which would bring in supplies towards paying off old scores, and which would help him to tide over the next term. Education under such conditions would have a deadening effect, or it would prove a discipline of the most bracing kind, fostering habits of independence and self-reliance. To Booker Washington it was of the latter kind. He formed good habits; he was a ready learner; he was thankful for any advice which those above him could impart. Reverence for Scripture is a very characteristic trait of the negro race; and the habit of reading daily a portion of the Bible which was formed at Hampton has never since been given up. While making progress at ordinary school or college work, he also added to his knowledge of certain outdoor industries, which was a valuable acquisition to be turned to account in future days. Then, the enlargement of his knowledge of human nature was likely to be of no small advantage to him. He may not have known before that the desire for education was so general among his own people, nor that the capacity for turning it to good account was so self-evident. He learned still further, that white men and women of social standing and high culture were willing to make personal self-sacrifices on behalf of the coloured race by becoming their teachers and their helpers. From such persons of culture and refinement he even learned the dignity of labour. He learned from their everyday example that education did not merely mean settling down into a more genteel life, but meant larger responsibilities and harder work. In other words, he came to see that the sharpening of the mental faculties was to ensure the hands working more efficiently, while it might be necessary to spend strength and talent for the benefit of others.

The all-round work at the Institute continued as it had begun. As regarded the general studies, every hour was turned to full account. The housework expected of the janitor was never either neglected or half done; and when each vacation time came round outside service had to be procured. During all this time both his mother and his brother stood by him, and not only gave him their sympathy, but all the help that was possible. At the present moment that brother, as well as a friend, who as a child was adopted by the family, are valued assistants in the Tuskegee Institution.

As the college course came to an end, and Booker Washington returned to his old haunts with their memories of coal mining and salt production, he was now a man of education to be looked up to and respected; and as the coloured people were ambitious of having a school established with a competent master, a fully-equipped graduate from Hampton Institute was no small acquisition. When the school was established the classes were soon crowded by those who, on account of their anxiety to improve, deserved to be distinguished as the most diligent and persevering of learners. There were a host of others also who, through having to attend to their daily labour were unable to attend school by day, were still not content to remain uninstructed in such good times as had dawned upon them. For these evening classes were provided, so that the tutor's time was occupied from early morning until late at night.

While at Malden he saw something of the doings of the members of the somewhat mysterious Ku-Klux Klan, which in the *Cyclopædia of Names* is thus described: — "A former secret organisation in the Southern United States, of which the object was to intimidate the negroes, carpet-baggers and 'scalawags,' and to prevent them from political action. It arose probably in 1867; was guilty of numerous outrages; and was suppressed in consequence of an Act of Congress — the Force Bill — passed in 1871." Street fights occurred, and the progress made since that day is seen in the fact that even the best part of the Southern public sentiment would not now tolerate the existence of such an association.

Had the policy of the Ku-Klux Klan been continued, and had public sympathy been accorded to its warfare, the cause of the negroes must have gone down until the race became a very genuine danger to the Government. The change in public opinion in the

South is not only one of the most cheering signs of the times, but many of Booker Washington's most earnest sympathisers and helpers are actually found in the former slave States. In the *Southern Letter* for May 1901, a little monthly newspaper which the founder of the Tuskegee Institution issues from his headquarters, a Southern lady of position, who was formerly a slave-owner, writes: —

> "God speed you in your noble work! Whenever I hear it said, 'The Caucasian blood in Booker Washington is the cause of his success and perseverance,' I answer, 'It is Principle.' I am a Southern white woman, once a slave-owner, educated to think it right, and to believe that coloured people could not provide for themselves, but would return to cannibalism if brought from under their masters, and so I thought it would be an awful thing for both races if they should be emancipated. I have long ago seen the folly of such opinions, and have seen that slavery was a horrible thing, and no one is more rejoiced than I am to see the progress and prosperity and enlightenment of the coloured people. Though a stranger in person, I am your true friend."

During the twelve years which followed the close of the Civil War, the Southern States were in a condition of unrest, which was natural, however, and was such as might have been expected after such a crisis as that which had shaken and threatened the very existence of the Republic. Considering what the relationship between the whites and the blacks had been, and what kind of traditional views the former had been trained to receive concerning the inferiority of the coloured race, we cannot wonder that the planters, and those who were with them, should have been appalled at the outlook. The situation became more anomalous, or even dangerous, through the mistakes of the Northern politicians, quite as much as through any want of charity, whether real or imaginary, on the part of the Southern statesmen. There were wounds to be healed on both sides, and there was too much of a disposition to maintain the vindictive war spirit after the war was over. Those who aimed at reconstruction certainly endangered their cause when they suddenly gave to the negroes greater political privileges than they understood, or would be able to use with any advantage to themselves. It would seem that some ludicrous instances occurred of even the lower kind of negroes being installed in important State offices. The result of this and many more indiscretions was naturally to foment feelings of great bitterness on both sides. If many in the North were disposed to make the emancipated slaves a bone of contention — a means of punishing the States which had wished to secede and to found a Commonwealth of their own — they missed their mark and involved the coloured race in much additional suffering which they might well have been spared. If we look through such a record as the autobiography of Laura Haviland, we find mention made of a number of atrocities belonging to this unsettled period of the kind which, under the circumstances, were pretty sure to happen. In a sense, Southern society was in a condition of that kind of chaos which has often marked similar transition periods. Never before were leaders more urgently needed who would work for peace and advancement by showing those, whose interests were supposed to be at variance, that their cause was one. Who could have prophesied at that time that the coloured people were destined to find some of their best friends among the whites of the south?

It has also to be confessed, that the outlook among the emancipated people themselves was such as might be expected to inspire misgiving, or even some alarm. They neither comprehended the situation nor could they properly understand what was the true aim of education. Booker Washington himself had been so thoroughly well trained in the best school that then existed, that of General Armstrong at the Hampton Institute, that he saw at a glance the kind of obstacles which threatened to bring disaster to his race by hindering their progress. In large measure the squalor and superstition which naturally come of generations of the darkest ignorance prevailed. It was seen that the training which was imperatively needed would have to be mainly industrial, while there must be no aspiration for equality with the whites by attempting to come into competition with them in the common avocations of everyday life. This was actually happening, however, so that while he studied for a time at Washington, the future founder of the great institute at Tuskegee saw that there were breakers ahead unless certain errors could be corrected. The negroes became too much disposed to look to the Government to make full provision for them, especially when they attained to the distinction of being able to read and write. Many would indulge in extravagant habits in order to make it appear that they were better off than they really were. Then there were an extraordinary number who aspired to the rare distinction of shining as divines and as admired preachers of the Gospel. Young men sought to become instructors of others before they had any ballast of character of their own. It was a time of danger and of the threatened loss of great opportunities, making it all the more remarkable that, in the way of social, educational and industrial progress, the negroes are where they are today. In those days of uncertainty the prophets of evil made their voices heard. As Booker Washington recently remarked in the *International Monthly*: "There were not a few who predicted that, as soon as the negro became a free man, he would not only cease to support himself and others, but he would become a tax upon the community." Persons who held notions of this kind doubtless supposed that negroes had some physical kinship with the native American Indians, who have never shown any disposition to take to field labour; and while they involve the Government in no small annual expense, their tribes are gradually dying out. The negroes, on the contrary, are fast multiplying, and their value as field labourers, and as workers in other departments of service, is a grateful contrast to the general incapacity of the Indians. In the article just referred to, Booker Washington is able to bear this high testimony to the general worth of his own people: —

"Few people in any part of our country have ever seen a black hand reached out from a street corner asking for charity. In our Northern communities a large amount of money is spent by individuals and municipalities in caring for the sick, the poor, and other classes of unfortunates. In the South, with very few exceptions, the negro takes care of himself, and of the unfortunate members of his race. This is usually done by a combination of individual members of the race, or through the churches or fraternal organisations. Not only is this true, but I want to make a story illustrate the condition that prevails in some parts of the South. The white people in a certain Black Belt county in the South had been holding a convention, the object of which was to encourage white people to emigrate into the county. After the adjournment of the convention an old coloured man met the president of the meeting on the street and asked the object of the convention. When told, the old coloured man replied, "Fore God, Boss, don't you know that we niggers have just as many white people in this county as we can support?""

The more we become acquainted with the general character and capacity of the negro, the more are we likely to become convinced that, instead of these people being any drawback to life in the South, those States, so favoured by Nature, could not do without them. It is true that a number of white persons in the States chiefly concerned have boldly testified that the coloured race have proved the best labourers which the country has ever had for its peculiar needs, and better than are likely to be forthcoming in the future. This fact is now being recognised by those whose interests are chiefly affected. Thus we even find it stated, "The greatest excitement and anxiety has been recently created among the white people in two counties in Georgia, because of the fact that a large proportion of the coloured people decided to leave. No stone has been left unturned to induce the coloured people to remain in the country and prevent financial ruin to many white farmers." The 8,900,000 bales of cotton grown in 1899, under free labour, is nearly fourfold greater than was produced in 1850 by slave labour.

During the transition or reconstruction time, especially during the period when he was completing his college training at Washington, Booker Washington was a keen observer of his own people, the result being that he probably understands their needs, idiosyncrasies and tendencies better than any other living authority. He also eagerly reads what others who are not members of his own race say upon the subject. What he considers the most valuable testimony under this head appeared about two years ago in an article in *Appleton's Popular Science Monthly*, written by Professor N. S. Shaler of Harvard University, and Dean of the Scientific School. Take this passage: —

"The negroes who came to North America had to undergo as complete a transition as ever fell to the lot of man, without the least chance to undergo an acclimatising process. They were brought from the hottest part of the earth to the region where the winter's cold is almost of arctic severity; from an exceedingly humid to a very dry air. They came to service under alien taskmasters, strange to them in speech and in purpose. They had to betake themselves to unaccustomed food, and to clothing such as they had never worn before. Rarely could one of the creatures find about him a familiar face of friend, parent or child, or an object that recalled his past life to him. It was an appalling change. Only those who know how the negro cleaves to all the dear, familiar things of life, how fond he is of life and friendliness, can conceive the physical and mental shock that this introduction to new conditions meant to them. To people of our own race it would have meant death. But these wonderful folk appear to have withstood the trials of their deportation in a marvellous way. They showed no particular liability to disease. Their longevity or period of usefulness was not diminished, or their fecundity obviously impaired. So far as I have been able to learn, nostalgia was not a source of mortality, as it would have been with any Aryan population. The price they brought in the market and the satisfaction of their purchasers with their qualities show that they were from the first almost ideal labourers."

When Booker Washington took up his residence in the town which the first President of the United States called the Federal City, but which was destined to take the name of that great patriot himself, a large number of negroes were found there. As a town, Washington has made wonderful strides since the close of the Civil War. The schools or colleges for coloured students, which are provided, of course have attraction for negroes, while other characteristics of the city also have strong fascination for such susceptible folk. If we may say so, in connection with a Republic, Washington is the seat of the Court and of the Legislature. The population may be a quarter of a million or more; but though not a very large town, it has recently developed into a beautiful place, fine buildings of wide thoroughfares and charming recreation grounds. Booker Washington seems to have discovered that such a place failed to exercise the best of influence on negro students. It is not in any sense an industrial centre; the people are for the most part Government officials, professional people, and persons of means who settle there because the surroundings and society are congenial. The temptation to coloured students was to assume too lofty airs, to despise any occupation other than a profession, and to think that the President and his Government were bound to find openings for them.

CHAPTER VI

AMERICAN INDIANS — WORK AT HAMPTON

Just about the time that he completed his education at the capital city, Booker Washington seems to have been tempted in a strange and unexpected way to give his life and energy to public speaking and politics. He took part in the agitation as a representative of a committee — which resulted in Charleston taking the place of Wheeling as capital of West Virginia. By effective platform work he no doubt was a chief agent in bringing about this change. Thus early, although he was hardly more than a youth himself, the future Professor of Tuskegee seems to have seen in what direction lay his pathway of life. Rightly guided, and taught to turn their energies and gifts to the best account, the negroes are a very capable race; but it was being proved on every hand that when left to go their own way without check or control they were liable to be captivated by very high-flown notions. As legislators, poets, jurists, artists and musicians their services were not pressingly in request; but in the world of a hundred industries there were magnificent openings for all who were adequately trained. It was fortunate both for himself and his own people that Booker Washington saw his opportunity and determined not to be diverted from it by any considerations of self-interest.

Under these conditions it was something like a special providence when he received an urgent message from General Armstrong asking him to revisit Hampton to address the students. It had become a custom for some one of the graduates who had passed through the institution to undertake this duty periodically, and the request was understood to be one of the greatest of compliments. The request was, of course, gladly complied with; and a revisit to the Institute showed that, under General Armstrong's capable and sympathetic control, the all-round educational work, and especially the industrial training, which was ever considered to be of first importance, had made great progress. The General had a quick eye to see where improvement could be introduced, and his energy never flagged. Until that time the negro race had not had such a friend, one who had a genius for seeing in what direction the coloured people would find that their best interests lay. Thus early he also probably saw that in his quondam pupil, Booker Washington, he had a comrade who was in every way fitted to extend the great enterprise. Certain students who had been prepared by this coloured tutor before being sent on to Hampton, had done exceedingly well, and this suggested that operations should be carried on in other directions.

It was characteristic of General Armstrong that he believed the American Indians, in common with the negroes, were capable of being raised to a condition of honour and usefulness by education and adequate training. The institute at Hampton was specially intended for Indians as well as for ex-slaves; and when it was decided to extend the accommodation for such pupils, where could so competent a teacher be found for them as Booker Washington? The acceptance on the part of the latter of such an office of course made it necessary for other connections of comparatively long standing to be severed, but the path of duty seemed to be clearly marked out, though the coloured pupils in the school in West Virginia would sorely miss their greatly-valued teacher.

Booker Washington's situation was now strangely anomalous. In their own eyes, and even in the eye of United States law, the Red folk were quite above those who happened to be black. In ante-emancipation days the Reds had actually been the owners of a number of Blacks as slaves. We believe that it may be assumed that even in the present day a Red man would be cordially welcomed at many hotels where negroes would be refused accommodation. Thus Booker Washington's large class of some scores of Indians would regard themselves as being socially quite superior to their tutor! A thoroughly well-educated negro had now to seek the improvement of a semi-wild assembly who might be disposed to resent such innovations as white people's civilisation suggested. Why should they have shorter hair? Why should the ancestral blanket be superseded by the conventional dress sanctioned by the United States President and the people he governed? On the whole, however, Booker Washington found these strange pupils to be amenable to reason; they were quite tractable when kindly treated.

The American Indians are an interesting nation of aborigines, and in course of an admirable article on their characteristics, habits and present condition, by Dr C. W. Greene, in *Chambers's Encyclopædia*, it is remarked that "their physical and mental characters are much the same from the Arctic Ocean to Fuegia." The tribes differ somewhat, some being devoted to hunting, according to the ancient, uncivilised way, others take to the tilling of the ground. One tribe may be warlike, another will be more effeminate, while both sexes appear to have a liking for athletic exercises. The following descriptive passage is borrowed from Dr Greene's article: —

"Their physical characters are a certain tallness and robustness, with an erect posture of the body; a skull narrowing from the eyebrows upward; prominence of the cheek-bones; the eyes black, deep-set, and having, it is thought, a slight tendency, in many cases, to strabismus; the hair coarse, very black, and perfectly straight; the nose prominent or even aquiline; the complexion usually of a reddish, coppery, or cinnamon colour, but with considerable variations in this respect. They have seldom much beard. In physical qualities the Indians thus make a somewhat close approximation to the Mongolian type. There is also a certain remarkable feebleness of constitution, combined, it may be, with vigour, suppleness and strength of body. At least, the aboriginal races do not resist well the epidemics introduced by the whites; and many tribes have been exterminated by the effects of the 'firewater' and the vicious habits brought in by more civilised men. The Red man is usually proud and reserved; serious, if not gloomy, in his views of life; comparatively indifferent to wit or pleasantry; vain of personal endowments; brave and fond of war, yet extremely cautious and taking no needless risks; fond of gambling and drinking; seemingly indifferent to pain; kind and hospitable to strangers, yet revengeful and cruel, almost beyond belief, to those who have given offence. . . . They often excel in horsemanship, and, as a rule, sight and hearing are wonderfully acute."

Such was the remnant of the aborigines whom Booker Washington now endeavoured to educate and to drill into civilised habits. A master difficulty consisted in teaching them the English language. All in the institute showed them great kindness and evidently won their gratitude. The strangest thing of all was that if the devoted tutor had occasion to go abroad with one of his pupils the Red man was eligible for reception anywhere, while in a steam-boat dining-room, or at the clerk's desk of an hotel, the Black one was ostracised. Apart from this there appeared to be some promise of success in the work of training the Indians; but it may be feared that through his kindness of heart their teacher harboured expectations which were too sanguine to be realised.

In the fall of 1900, as he himself explains in course of an article on "The Economic Value of the Negro," in *The International Monthly* for December of that year, Booker Washington received letters showing that openings for negro labourers existed in Cuba, the Sandwich Islands and elsewhere. This naturally led him to think closely on the subject mentioned, and to compare the negro with the Red race, *e.g.*: —

"When the first twenty slaves were landed at Jamestown, Virginia, in 1619, it was this economic value which caused them to be brought to this country. At the same time that these slaves were being brought to the shores of Virginia from their native land, Africa, the woods of Virginia were swarming with thousands of another dark-skinned race. The question naturally arises, Why did the importers of negro slaves go to the trouble and expense to go thousands of miles for a dark-skinned people, to hew wood and draw water for the whites, when they had right about them a people of another race who could have answered this purpose? The answer is that the Indian was tried and found wanting in the commercial qualities which the negro seemed to possess. The Indian would not submit to slavery as a race, and in those instances where he was tried as a slave his labour was not profitable, and he was found unable to stand the physical strain of slavery. As a slave, the Indian died in large numbers. This was true in San Domingo and other parts of the American continent. . . . The Indian refused to submit to bondage and to learn the white man's ways. The result is that the greater portion of American Indians have disappeared, and the greater portion of those who remain are not civilised. The negro, wiser and more enduring than the Indian, patiently endured slavery; and the contact with the white man has given the negro in America a civilisation vastly superior to that of the Indian."

To this may be added the testimony of Professor Shaler, of Harvard University, in *Appleton's Popular Science Monthly*: — "If we compare the Algonquin Indian, in appearance a sturdy fellow, with these negroes, we see of what stuff the blacks are made. A touch of housework and of honest toil took the breath of the aborigines away, but these tropical exotics fell to their tasks and trials far better than the men of our own kind could have done."

It has also to be remembered that the nearly ten million negroes in the Southern States show that the total has more than doubled since the close of the Civil War, and are still capable of being turned to vast profitable account. The Indians show a decrease, and cost the Government about £2,500,000 a year.

The attention thus given to the Indians' school at Hampton was an interesting passage in Booker Washington's experience; but even while that work was in progress he was gradually drifting into the course which would represent the main service of his life. When the discoverers of America first came in contact with the Red Men they may have thought them to be superior to the negroes; but from that day to this they have practically made no progress, and today appear to be more than ever a dying nation. It was quite in keeping with the philanthropic General Armstrong to attempt to befriend and raise such tribes, but even he must have realised how vastly greater was the return in the case of the negroes.

As has been shown, in the years which followed the general emancipation, the coloured people showed the most eager desire to obtain some kind of education. It happened that at Hampton there was a large number outside of the Institute who were of this class, and when it was resolved to found a night school for their benefit Booker Washington was requested to undertake its superintendence. These evening classes were to be a kind of preparatory school for such as might afterwards attend the day school of the Institute, and the conditions of their receiving two hours' nightly instruction were sufficiently onerous to deter any from coming forward but the most determined enthusiasts. A long, hard day's work had to be fulfilled before they could think of joining their class. It is no wonder that such scholars are now doing well in the world. The school is still continued at Hampton, but the scholars have increased from tens to hundreds.

So far throughout the course of his working life Booker Washington has never lost faith in his own people, and, while using his opportunities to benefit them, no hard-working leader has ever had fewer disappointments. While American politicians, sometimes with bated breath, have been talking about the problems of the Southern Black Belt, this far-sighted negro has clearly seen that ten millions of the coloured race in the wide territory of the South is rather an advantage to be thankful for than "a problem" to create dismay. How readily the young negro men and women can adapt themselves to circumstances, and benefit others of their own race while making a position for themselves, is constantly being proved. The fact is confirmed by many independent witnesses hailing from different quarters. We close this chapter by another passage on this subject by Professor Shaler, in *Appleton's Popular Science Monthly*, and quoted, with admiration, by Booker Washington himself in *The International Monthly*: —

"Moreover, the production of good tobacco requires much care, which extends over about a year from the time the seed is planted. Some parts of the work demand a measure of judgment such as intelligent negroes readily acquire. They are, indeed, better fitted for the task than white men, for they are commonly more interested in their task than whites of the labouring class. The result was that, before the period of the revolution, slavery was firmly established in the tobacco planting colonies of Maryland, Virginia and North Carolina; it was already the foundation of their only considerable industry. . . . This industry (cotton), even more than that of raising tobacco, called for abundant labour which could be absolutely commanded and severely tasked in the season of extreme heats. For this work the negro proved to be the only fit man, for, while the whites can do the work, they prefer other employment. Thus it came about that the power of slavery in this country became rooted in its soil. The facts show that, based on an ample foundation of experience, the judgment of the Southern people was to the effect that this creature of the tropics was a better labourer in their fields than the men of their own race.

"Much has been said about the dislike of the white man for work in association with negroes. The failure of the whites to have a larger share in the agriculture of the South has been attributed to this cause. This seems to be clearly an error. The dislike to the association of races in labour is, in the slaveholding States, less than in the North. There can be no question that, if the Southern folk could have made white labourers profitable, they would have preferred to employ them, for the reason that the plantations would have required less fixed capital for their operation. The fact was, and is, that the negro is there a better labouring man in the field than the white. Under the conditions he is more enduring, more contented and more trustworthy than the men of our own race."

The negroes have many qualities such as are sure to heighten their value in the eyes of employers and business men. On the whole, they are a contented race when fairly used. We can hardly think of them as becoming political agitators. They know too well where their interest lies to favour strikes, and so become the victims of those who professionally foment them. It would also seem that they generally contract a kind of affection for those who employ them and who use them well. Complaint is made of more crime showing itself among negroes in certain centres; but when it is considered that only a generation ago the whole race was in bondage, the wonder is that so little crime has been manifest. Provide good schools and an industrial training, and the coloured folk will prove to be a law-abiding race.

CHAPTER VII

THE BEGINNING OF A LIFE WORK

The singular way in which Booker Washington proceeded from one thing to another, until, at length, he found himself beginning the great work of his life before he was himself quite aware of the fact, strongly tends to prove that he was destined to be a leader of his own people. We believe that he would himself acknowledge that the chain of circumstances which led up to his being landed at Tuskegee in 1881 was entirely providential. He did not himself seek the opening; it came to him unsought at a time when his services were still urgently needed at Hampton, where he had become General Armstrong's right-hand man, or his most efficient assistant. He was still fully occupied with the large class of Indian boys during the day, and then, until a late hour every night, with the more enthusiastic coloured pupils of his own people. At the same time, he was pursuing his own studies for self-improvement with characteristic ardour. Probably neither the good General Armstrong nor this chief officer of his staff as yet thought the arrangements at the Institute, which were found to work so well, were other than permanent.

A great change, which was nothing less than a great forward movement, was at hand, however. It came to pass that, at a time when he was least expecting it, the General received an urgent message for help from the darkest part of the Black Belt of Alabama. The missive in question came from white people, who were genuine friends of the negroes, and, as such, were representative of large numbers of others in the Southern States who were like minded. It occurred to these good souls that a large proportion of the coloured people — admirable human material, if turned to good account — was running to waste through lack of that knowledge which could only come of education or training suitable to their needs. The blacks greatly outnumbered the whites, and by very many their capacities for service to the State were not understood. It was thought by those who had put themselves in communication with General Armstrong that an institute, similar to the one which had proved so successful at Hampton, might be founded in the little town of Tuskegee, which stood aside from the main railway line, but had a branch for its accommodation. It had not entered into anybody's day-dreams to suppose that anyone, save an accomplished white man, would be competent to undertake so arduous an enterprise; but when the General received the application, and had thought about it, he clearly saw, to his own satisfaction, that Booker Washington was the man most likely to make such a school as the one suggested a success. The following passage from an open letter in the *Century Magazine* for September 1895, by Mr G. T. Speed, affords some notion of what the general outlook was in Alabama at the date in question: —

"When the attention of philanthropists was first directed to the ignorant condition of the freedmen in the South, in nine cases out of ten the practical effort to do something for their improvement was controlled by clergymen, and was largely influenced by sentimental considerations. The chief object seemed to be to grow a great crop of negro preachers, lawyers and doctors. The result was so disheartening that, fifteen years after the war was over, there were grave doubts whether the coloured race in the South was not lapsing into a barbarism worse than that of slavery. Fortunately, among those educators and philanthropists there was at least one sane man, the late General S. C. Armstrong, of Hampton. His main idea was to train workmen and teachers. Mr Washington was one of these teachers. Of him and his work General Armstrong, shortly before his death, said: — 'It is, I think, the noblest and grandest work by any coloured man in the land. What compares with it in general value and power for good? It is on the Hampton plan, combining labour and study, commands high respect from both races, flies no denominational flag, but is earnestly and thoroughly Christian, is out of debt, well managed and organised.'"

Concerning the opinions, the aims and aspirations of General Armstrong's disciple, the same friend says: —

"Mr Booker T. Washington had become persuaded that most of the efforts at training his people in purely academic directions were almost entirely thrown away. He held that the time was not ripe, and his people were not prepared for the higher scholastic training of which the Greek and Latin classics are the basis, but that they needed to be taught how to work to advantage in the trades and handicrafts, how to be better farmers, how to be more thrifty in their lives, and, most of all, how to resist the money-lender's inducements to mortgage their crops before they were made. It was with these great ideas that he began his work at Tuskegee."

When Booker Washington acceded to General Armstrong's request to proceed to Tuskegee to give practical shape to the white people's wishes, he received as many good wishes and congratulations as if he was going to accept an enviable appointment in some already founded and flourishing institution. The fact was, however, that not even the straw was as yet gathered for the bricks with which the proposed school would have to be built. Not even a site had been chosen, and no one knew where this might be found. The most favourable features of the situation were that the coloured folk were very desirous of obtaining some education, while the whites were equally anxious that a school should be provided for them. The cordial greeting accorded to the newcomer on every hand was perhaps more flattering than reassuring; for the obstacles in the way of success seemed so formidable that even the sanguine and persevering Booker Washington might have been excused had he hesitated. Had he not been a negro, he would probably have declared that the task assigned to him was impossible.

The blighting effects of the Civil War were still visible; and when a beginning at teaching was actually made, the class had to be content with the accommodation of a tumble-down kind of building which was a very imperfect protection from the weather. In some respects the ex-slaves appeared to be no better off than when they were in bondage. In order to become acquainted with the people, and to understand their general condition and in what degree an effort to raise them promised to succeed, it was necessary to visit them in their homes in the surrounding country. In the main, their cabins showed no improvement on those in which they had been housed in the days of slavery; and some of their habits were as comical on the one hand as they were improvident on the other. Practically what we call one-room life was, in a great number of instances, a chief obstacle to their more complete civilisation. While in need of better homesteads and of many necessary but commonplace things, either for use or ornament, which they were, through their ignorance, quite unable to turn to any account. Their ignorance also led to superstition and to one-sided views of things, which suggested mischievous action. False pride would naturally inspire a love of showing off, which meant a waste of resources, which, in the hands of better economists, would have gone far towards providing the family with the comforts of life.

The school teaching commenced just after midsummer, 1881; and the number of the students who came was at once as many as could be accommodated, and their eagerness to learn testified to the earnest desire for education which was common among the coloured race. Had all been taken who wished to come, the school would have been a very large one at the outset; but at first the plan was to take only those who were not mere children and who had already acquired some learning. Some who sat in the classes were even approaching middle-age. Perhaps a chief drawback was that the aims of the teacher and the expectations of the learners did not generally agree. As Mr Speed tells us, Booker Washington's capital originally consisted of "nothing but ideas, ambition and a few friends, none of whom could do much in the way of contributions." His ideas were worth more than gold, however; while his friends were of sterling quality, one being an ex-slaveholder, who had done more than anyone else in originating the school. It may seem to be strange that some of the best and shrewdest friends of negroes in the Southern States at the present time are ex-slave-owners. Others among the white people would have preferred that the old-time hewers of wood and drawers of water for the superior race should remain illiterate, thinking that their coming in contact with books would have the effect of marring their capacity for field service. Not a few, especially at that time, in common with the coloured people themselves, entirely misapprehended in what an effective education consisted. It was too often supposed that it meant mere book-learning that would release its possessors from hard, manual labour. To General Armstrong and Booker Washington education would be of value to negroes because it would enable them to do more effectively the labour connected with a number of important industries to which they were called. This obvious truth is far better understood than it was a quarter of a century ago. The work done at Hampton, at Tuskegee, and at the many schools on a similar basis which have since sprung up in the Southern States, has not only demonstrated that the negro race may be made to become a source of vast good or profit to the Republic, it has revolutionised public opinion.

Meanwhile the numbers actually under instruction, and also of those who were exceedingly anxious to enter the classes, increased daily. At the same time, the overwhelming need of the coloured race, and the great opportunities to raise them which offered themselves, made a deep impression on Booker Washington, as it also did on one who was thus early an able and sympathetic helper in the work — Miss Olivia Davidson, afterwards Mrs Booker Washington. The latter was a superior girl, of coloured ancestry, although personally she was as white as the most pure-blooded descendant of the Pilgrim Fathers that could have been found. These two kindred souls were now one in the work, and, of course, they had many anxious consultations. It did not seem as though the work of the school could continue to be carried on in the forsaken church and half-ruinous shed which so far had been the only accommodation.

A short distance outside of the town there was an old plantation of a hundred acres, and as the house had been burned down, this was to be secured for the low price of a hundred dollars. If it could possibly be effected, the removal of the school to such a site promised to be a great step in advance; and, after overcoming a good many difficulties, a portion of the money was borrowed and possession was obtained. Having made such a good beginning, it seemed to be impossible not to go forward, especially when the enthusiasm of the coloured people was encouraged by the hearty sympathy and practical help of the whites. The fact is that, in proportion as the schools prospered, both blacks and whites were being made to see that they had very much in common; and friends of the negro will gladly recognise that the continued aid of friends in the Southern States has made uninterrupted progress possible. The next thing was to put up a main school building at a cost of six thousand dollars, the students themselves being the builders. For some time after this the difficulty in obtaining adequate funds was a cause of great anxiety; but what at the time seemed to be unsurmountable obstacles were always overcome, and the way was then open for still further advances. The first year's work at Tuskegee was, on the whole, a time of preparation and of founding what was destined to become a distinguished institute on a solid basis. It was then that Booker Washington set up a home of his own, into which he was able to receive his teaching staff. He was united in marriage to Miss Fannie Smith, who, like himself, had been trained at Hampton. In less than two years the first Mrs Washington died, leaving an infant daughter. In this early stage of the work, distinguished aid continued to be given by Miss Davidson in collecting, in giving shrewd advice, and in other service, including that of teaching. As will be made to appear, from this date the progress made and the growth of the Institute was no less rapid than wonderful.

But while the work was thus extending, the question came to be asked, even by intelligent and far-seeing people, Is not industrial education for negroes a craze? The majority were convinced that industrial training in this case needed to go hand-in-hand with book-learning. It was thought that men should understand farming and divers handicrafts, and that women should possess such accomplishments as cooking, sewing and dressmaking, and other domestic matters. Other friends of the negro, who in the main agreed with this policy, still thought that there was danger of its being pushed too far, in which case the movement might even develop into a craze, and then it was almost certain that the outcome would be "a less extended and thorough mental and moral culture." In an open letter in the *Century Magazine* for 1889, Mr S. W. Powell referred to such objections: —

> "The proposed change implies too great a concession to the widely prevalent opinion that the negro is, and in the nature of the case must be, better fitted for manual than for mental labour. They argue also that the new departure tends to foster materialistic notions of the value of education, the main object of which should be the ennoblement of the worker rather than the production of more cotton, sugar, coal, iron or lumber. . . . Then, again, the surprising success in some schools, and notably in one, in mastering the more advanced branches is profoundly affecting the opinions of many of the most influential people in the South as to the capacity of the negro, and to do anything which would make the work in these brigade schools less extensive, or less thorough, will push him and his friends off this hard-won vantage-ground."

Still further, we are exhorted to remember that "leaders qualified to hold their own in the sharp competition of professional life are a great, if not the greatest, need of the coloured race in this country. Over wide areas most of their clergy are illiterate, immoral, self-seeking, bitter sectarians, and the most determined opponents of every kind of improvement. So, too, the lack of lawyers, editors and physicians of sufficiently broad and thorough training to be able to defend their weaker brethren against designers or incapable advisers is a very discouraging feature of the situation. The negroes do not, as a rule, seek the leadership or counsel of competent and honest whites in matters of religion or of business, hence the greater need of well-qualified men of their own race."

It need hardly be emphasised that those who are favouring the cause of industrial education, as a means best calculated to raise the coloured race, are quite as earnest in their desire for negroes to advance to higher culture when exceptional capacity shows itself. In the nature of things, however, this higher culture can be extended only to a comparatively few individuals. Referring to those who are unable to push their way so far, and yet are aiming at becoming scholars, Mr Powell adds: —

> "If they had the industrial education now given in some schools they might support themselves in the same communities where they teach, acquiring decent homes of their own, which would be a much-needed example and

incentive to all about them. The lack of anything worthy to be called home is the most appalling obstacle to the elevation of the negro. If these higher schools should furnish this industrial training, as some of them are beginning to do, nine-tenths, or, in many cases, nineteen-twentieths, of the pupils who never finish even the grammar-school course might be put in the way of living for the rest of their lives like human beings instead of like beasts."

The fact is, that the industrial training is not only becoming more widely recognised as being what the coloured people most urgently need, it tends largely to make the students more independent by placing them in a situation in which they can pay their own way instead of receiving outside aid. Then, while the negroes have splendid capacities for service, there is surely no other people who so greatly need to be made to realise the value and dignity of labour. As Mr Powell further says: —

"It was one of the greatest evils of slavery that manual labour was considered degrading. This was especially mischievous in its effects on the poor whites. The South is only slowly coming to believe that one who works for a living can be qualified for good society. In many of the industrial schools already established, students are beginning to take pride in their command of tools, in their well-planned and executed mechanical work, and in the thorough, clean tillage, the enlarged and varied products, and the improved stock and buildings of the farms attached to these schools. . . . The ability to plan or build a church, a schoolhouse, or a dwelling, or to carry on a farm as it should be carried on, gives a man's opinion about purely professional matters greater weight in all struggling communities. A teacher, minister or physician could hardly have, aside from his mental and moral qualities, a more effective passport to the confidence and respect of coloured people."

It was well both for himself no less than for those who were dependent upon him for guidance and education, that Booker Washington harboured the notions he did concerning the worth of labour. Anyone who had visited the institution he was building up at Tuskegee, during the first and second year of its struggling existence, would have seen that if the work eventually succeeded order would have to be brought out of chaos. This was emphatically true of all things connected with the daily life of the students on the estate; but beyond that the hereditary prejudices of the students and their family connections had to be overcome. There seems to have been a deeply rooted opinion that, if school learning did not lift a man up above the necessity to labour, it was hardly worth having. Parents and students alike tenaciously held this notion, so that, besides looking after his growing institute, Booker Washington had to travel about the State of Alabama to show that such prejudices were no less false than mischievous. At the same time he had what would generally be regarded as his own prejudices, but, come what would, he was determined to hold his idea, and to give it practical expression. When buildings had to be put up on the estate, he took care that none save the students themselves should have any hand in building them. These coloured aspirants had even to dig the clay, to make and burn the bricks that were needed; and it was only after three dismal failures in trying to form a kiln on scientific principles that this enterprise, which demanded exhausting labour, was crowned with success. As was to be expected, some of the students grew discouraged while undergoing such experience; but those who persevered and conquered with their leader at last found themselves braced or strengthened, rather than injured, by the difficulties which they had been enabled to conquer. At the present time the students at Tuskegee are competent to turn out 100,000 bricks of superior quality a month, and all of the forty buildings on the ground are their own work. The latest addition in this department is a magnificent library building, the gift of Mr Andrew Carnegie, which, in the *Southern Letter* of December 1901, was spoken of as "now being rushed to completion." This house has cost Mr Carnegie £4000, and when finished there was already a large collection of books waiting to be placed on its shelves.

In proportion as the students increased in the early days of the Tuskegee Institute, there came the urgent need for additional buildings and more money, both for providing these and for the general outlay. It was decided to put up a main building at a cost of £2000, and in order to raise money Booker Washington had to do a good deal of travelling as a collector. He found the rich quite willing to respond in a handsome way when his needs became known; but while the work has often been stimulated by large gifts, the more numerous small gifts of commonplace people have from the first been its mainstay. Practically he was introduced to the people of the Northern States by General Armstrong, who accompanied him on a collecting tour. On this and other occasions some striking adventures were met with, and all tended to show that hard work, perseverance and freedom from worry carried a man over a great deal of ground, while in a providential way all things seemed in the end to turn out for the best. Booker Washington had the gift of being able to impart some of his own energy and enthusiasm to his subordinates, and even to the students, who generally came round to see in what direction their best interests lay. A wholesome discipline was maintained throughout the institution, and thus, while being qualified to become instructors of their fellows of the coloured race, the students learned to love and to respect their leader.

CHAPTER VIII

SOME ACTUAL RESULTS — POSSIBLE DEVELOPMENTS

In the ordinary sense, neither General Armstrong nor Booker Washington would have been put down as a statesman; but, of course, each had his own individual sentiments as a citizen of the Republic. Thus each was well aware that both the North and the South had to deal with a population problem of an exceptionally difficult kind. The North had an unceasing tide of foreign immigration; the South had its Black Belt and a negro population, which appeared to be competent to double itself in course of a generation. General Armstrong was as large-hearted a friend of the coloured race as could have been found, and he appears to have protested against "either coddling the blacks or hampering the whites" on the part of the North. In an article in *The International Monthly* on the Southern question, Mr Edward P. Clark tells us that General Armstrong "opposed alike Federal Election Laws, designed and administered in the interest of the blacks, and Federal Education Laws, appropriating money for the South in the same interest. He urged that a negro could never become an ordinary citizen until he should cease to be the 'ward of the nation.'" Booker Washington appears to hold views on this matter which essentially are in close agreement with the policy of his late master. *E.g.*: —

"General Armstrong did not regard it as a serious misfortune for the negro that he was discouraged and even prevented from voting. He condemned unfair methods, but he believed that the cure of such methods might and should be left to local public sentiment. Mr Washington opposes unjust race legislation, like the recent proposition in Georgia to disfranchise the black man, as a black man; but he does not urge the negroes in his own State of Alabama to make voting the chief end of life. The keynote of the advice given by both of these leaders to the negro always has been to make himself a good citizen, worthy to share in the government of town, State and Republic, and trust to his white neighbour to recognise his right to such share when that time should come. 'Be a voter, and then think about being a man'; that was long the only watchword of the Northern Republican politician for the negro. 'Be a man, and then think about being a voter'; such is the message to him from the Armstrongs and the Washingtons."

Mr Clark adds this cheerful note: —

"It is easy enough to make a catalogue of outrage and injustice upon the Southern blacks, so long and gloomy as to justify a feeling of profound discouragement regarding the future. The most hopeful feature of the situation is the fact that those friends and champions of the negro who have studied the question most carefully upon the spot, have grown more confident all the time that ultimately things would work out right. General Armstrong died full of faith in the future. Mr Washington grows more hopeful every year. Outsiders may well feel that there is no occasion for despair when the voice of cheer is heard from the very heart of the Black Belt."

We learn from an article by Mr Pitt Dillingham, in *The Outlook* of New York (April 12, 1902), that Booker Washington is a trustee of the Calhoun Coloured School in Lowndes County, a part of the Black Belt in Alabama, where the negroes greatly outnumber the whites. The school may possibly take its name from the family of John Caldwell Calhoun (1782-1850), a well-remembered statesman of the Republic, who was Vice-President 1825-1832; an uncompromising defender of slavery, and propounder of the political doctrine of Nullification — the rejection of any State of any Act which was judged to be unconstitutional. The students in the Calhoun School receive just such an industrial education as would be given at Hampton or Tuskegee; but to us the institution is the more noteworthy because it has become identified with a kind of land-movement, which may have the most far-reaching consequences, so far as the coloured race is concerned. Practically, the school is an illustration of the way in which those who have been trained at Hampton, or under Booker Washington at Tuskegee, in turn become teachers and leaders to their own people. Mr Dillingham remarks: —

"The two young women from New England — one from Boston, one from New Haven — Hampton teachers who first rang a school-bell ten years ago on the old Shelby plantation in Lowndes County, simply desired to get into the Black Belt, to identify themselves with a community of cotton-raisers as neighbours, to know the people at first hand, and then to meet the human need about them in any way possible; above all, helping the people to help themselves . . . in the Black Belt of Alabama, a county containing the largest proportion of blacks to whites. The average ratio for the seventeen counties in Alabama's cotton-belt is less than three to one. In Lowndes County in 1892 the ratio was seven to one — 28,000 to 4000. This meant maximum conditions of ignorance and poverty — a county likely to be Africanised if it could not be Americanised."

The school at Calhoun had 300 students, and its land extended over 100 acres. As there were such great opportunities, if the right means were taken to secure them, the teachers were moved by a desire to provide openings for their students in the county instead of their being obliged to seek uncertain employment in the distance. Why not buy land and divide it into small holdings, which even negroes could purchase for their own? That would be to show practical sympathy with the native sentiment — "I always did want to own something that wouldn't die; your mule, he'll die, but the land is gwine to live."

That idea gained favour; it was strictly in accordance with the negro's economic programme; and thus, when a plantation of nearly 1100 acres was purchased and was divided into over twenty farms, the enterprise was well in hand. In time other estates were purchased; the movement, which is favoured by the whites and ex-planters, is so extremely popular with the blacks that "one man recently sent five cents ten miles by a friend to go towards his farm!" As might be expected, all this has not been carried out without there being some failure and discouragement, but, on the whole, the movement has realised the hopes of its promoters. Mr Dillingham adds: —

> "On the economic side, Calhoun's scheme means buying a plantation at wholesale price, and breaking up the plantation into small farms, by a group of men who make advance payments and then finish buying by paying rent for a term of years. The fifty-acre farm means a basis for a new agriculture or intensive farming, also sharp, individual responsibility of buyer, plus family life and labour and friendly co-operation of a neighbourhood. The plantation, with its 'quarters' and renters and croppers, who 'stay' to make and pick crops, but have no home — the plantation, the old, before-the-war, economic unit, is transformed into an American neighbourhood of farms and homes, within sound of church and bell. This is the light set on the hill."

This is how the work, commenced at Hampton and Tuskegee,

can develop or expand; and, while benefiting the State, is also found to bring the white people and the coloured race into friendly contact, the former doing what lies in their power to advance the cause. Thriving neighbourhoods of coloured people promise to come into existence, for "the South is not shutting the industrial door, or the educational door, or the church or the house door on the negro."

There are doubtless persons in the Republic who are disposed to think that, so far as education is concerned, Nashville, the capital and largest town of Tennessee, is the paradise of the negroes. The place is famous for its schools, churches and colleges, Fisk College and some others ranking as universities. The coloured race are in the minority. The fact tends to promote their own peace and happiness, that they are not overmuch fascinated by politics; and, according to common report, the coloured people in the town are more eager than others to obtain an education. Three great colleges, one named after Roger Williams, have been founded for their special benefit. A certain small proportion of negroes may advance to higher scholarship, but the main part do not get beyond what used to be called grammar-learning; while it is a most happy thing, both for whites and blacks, that the industrial programme of General Armstrong and Booker Washington is in large measure carried out. As a writer in the *Century Magazine* remarks: —

> "All boarding pupils are required to devote an hour a day to such forms of labour as may be required of them, and the cleanest school building I ever saw is Livingstone Hall of Fisk University, which is kept clean by the pupils. A certain number of young men at Fisk learn printing every year, and others will henceforth learn carpentry and other useful handicrafts; while the young women are taught nursing the sick and the rules of hygiene, cooking, dressmaking and plain sewing. The course of industrial training in Central Tennessee College and Roger Williams University is about the same."

The majority of those who are thus educated become teachers of their own people, and in this service there are plenty of openings for them. The negroes seem to be as amenable to the civilising influences of education as any race with whom they might be compared, and in Nashville they are peculiarly fortunate in their teachers. You may meet with thriving negro business men whose honesty and tact are much commended by the whites. They see that the acquisition of property gives them a good standing in the world, so that they may sometimes need a little wholesome advice to check their excessive eagerness to become rich. Then the character of their well-furnished and comfortable houses shows how completely they have been raised from the squalid one-room life of their former cabins. "These well-kept houses," says one who visited a number of them in the town for purposes of inspection, "are not only the best proof of the progress in civilisation of the negro race, but they are also the best security for the welfare of the whites in property and in morals, and I have never had so much hope for the future of this region as since I learned these things. Granted that these may be the picked few, it is most hopeful that there is a picked few, whose example will inspire others to lift themselves up." In proportion as they advance they show commendable enthusiasm for embarking in philanthropic enterprise. Thus, as a writer in the *Century Magazine* tells us: —

> "The only negro church publishing-house in the world" is located at Nashville, a large building five storeys high. "It was purchased with the contributions of the children of the African Methodist Episcopal Church. A home for aged and indigent negroes is the latest enterprise, while a shop for teaching mechanical trades was opened. . . . The number of church societies is, of course, legion."

All this shows how far-reaching was the influence of such institutes as Tuskegee and Hampton, when their methods were thus copied. To come back to Booker Washington's own work, however, we find that at the end of fourteen years the two old buildings in which he had commenced in 1881 had given place to forty buildings on an estate of two thousand acres. At that time there were rented fifteen cottages not on the school estate, while many of the teachers had houses of their own. The annual cost was then under £15,000, the number of persons to be supported exceeding a thousand. It is not often that the students are able to pay wholly for their board; and at the time in question less than £2000 in the year was received under this head. Various funds, including a grant from the State, supplied near £2000 annually. The cost of each student is £10 a year, board being paid for partly in money and partly in labour. £40 suffices one to complete the four years' course, while a sum of £200 provides a permanent scholarship. A carpenter, a bricklayer, or a blacksmith must, under all circumstances, pass some part of each day in the school. The aim is to have all well taught, and to inspire a laudable ambition, hoping to excel and to succeed by hard work, perseverance and honest, upright lives. The training is also partly religious, for to come short of that would not yield satisfaction to the negro. The following from the article by Mr Speed, already referred to, gives a word-picture of what takes place on a high public day at Tuskegee, when friends from far and near assemble to see and hear what is being done not only in the schools, but by those who also represent the thirty or more industries which are carried on: —

> "At the commencement, held at the end of May, the exercises included not only music and speaking, but an exhibition of the handiwork of the pupils, who were called on to show how each kind of work was done. One showed the method of putting tires on a buggy, another the construction of a house, another the pinning of the same, and still another the painting of the structure; the girls showed the process of ironing a shirt, of cleaning and lighting a lamp, of making bread, cake and pie, of cutting and fitting a dress, and so on. Other boys illustrated wheelwrighting, bricklaying, plastering, mattress-making, printing, and various agricultural processes. To the crowds of interested negroes at this commencement this seemed something worth while, because it was practical and within the range of their own experience and attainment. . . . Among all the educational efforts among the negroes there is probably none more interesting, wise or successful than this work of Mr Washington's at Tuskegee."

To understand what progress has been made, we have to contrast the present outlook with that of forty years ago, when negroes were considered to be incapable of living as free people with credit to themselves, and when certain States actually had laws prohibiting their being set free.

CHAPTER IX

CONTINUED PROGRESS —
POPULARITY AS A SPEAKER

While the now great institution at Tuskegee continued to grow and to increase in popularity both with the North and the South, there seemed to be no reason for departure in any measure from the course marked out by General Armstrong. The number as well as the need of the negroes was so great that preparatory classes, similar to those which had succeeded so well at Hampton, were arranged for, and candidates eagerly came forward for admission — young people whose mettle was sufficiently well tested by their having to get through a long, hard day's work before they could enjoy the privilege and luxury of some hours of teaching in the night school. This kind of service has grown, and at the present time there are probably not far short of 500 pupils in its classes. Of course many advance from this stage to get admitted to the day school of the Institute.

All along Booker Washington has been subjected to the temptation to excel in public speaking, but he has indulged in this only so far as the practice would advance his work. He began to make his mark when he gave an address before the Educational Association at Madison, the capital of Wisconsin, and the seat of a university. Whenever he spoke the founder of Tuskegee Institute was recognised as a gifted, natural orator; and his most famous address, and one which was destined to have most far-reaching consequences, while it added to the popularity of the man and his work, was one which he gave in the autumn of 1895 at a Cotton States Exhibition, which was also to some extent international.

This great show was held at Atlanta, the capital of Georgia, a great railway centre, and a place of much trade and manufacture. It has also a university for coloured students. The crowded assembly on such an occasion was largely representative of the most influential people among the whites both in the North and the South, as well as those of the negro race. It was an exciting time, and quidnuncs of all parties were eagerly anticipating what the dark-skinned professor would say. Of course the note he struck was one which tended to the doing away of racial differences. All along Booker Washington has been honest in his convictions and in his manner of giving utterance to them. Where wrong is seen to exist he is brave enough to speak of it. He has even been so honestly outspoken in regard to the shortcomings of his own people as to earn their resentment, until it was found that what was said was true, and was no symptom of want of sympathy. Those who listened to the address at Atlanta would be impressed with his profound sympathy with his own coloured race, with the high value he set upon their possible achievements, and with his passionate representations of the interests which the white and coloured race had in common, each being thus dependent on the other. The address was the chief thing which took place in connection with the Exhibition, and Booker Washington received an autograph letter from President Cleveland thanking him for having said what he did. A few passages from *The World's* account of what actually occurred may best enable us to realise the scene: —

"While President Cleveland was waiting at Grey Gables to send the electric spark that started the machinery of the Atlanta Exposition, a negro Moses stood before a great audience of white people and delivered an oration that marks a new epoch in the history of the South. . . . When Professor Booker T. Washington . . . stood on the platform of the auditorium, with the sun shining over the heads of his auditors into his eyes, and his whole face lit up with the fire of prophecy, Clark Howell, the successor of Henry Grady, said to me, 'That man's speech is the beginning of a moral revolution in America. It is the first time that a negro has made a speech in the South on any important occasion before an audience composed of white men and women.' It electrified the audience, and the response was as if it had come from the throat of a whirlwind. . . . All this time the eyes of the thousands present looked straight at the negro orator. A strange thing was to happen. A black man was to speak for his people, and with none to interrupt him. As Professor Washington strode to the edge of the stage, the low, descending sun shot fiery rays through the windows into his face. A great shout greeted him. He turned his head to avoid the blinding light, and moved about the platform for relief. Then he turned his wonderful countenance without a blink of the eyelids and began to speak. There was a remarkable figure — tall, bony, straight as a Sioux chief, high forehead, straight nose, heavy jaws, and strong, determined mouth, with big, white teeth, piercing eyes and a commanding manner. The sinews stood out on his bronzed neck, and his muscular right arm swung high in the air, with a lead pencil grasped in the clenched fist. His big feet were planted squarely, with the heels together and the toes turned out. His voice rang out clear and true, and he paused impressively as he made each point. Within ten minutes the multitude was in an uproar of enthusiasm — handkerchiefs were waved, canes were flourished, hats were tossed in the air. The fairest women in Georgia stood up and cheered. It was as if the orator had bewitched them. And when he held his dusky hand high above his head, with the fingers stretched wide apart, and said to the white people of the South on behalf of his race, 'In all things that are purely social we can be separate as the fingers, yet one as the hand in all things essential to mutual progress,' the great wave of applause dashed itself against the walls, and the whole audience was on its feet in a delirium of applause, and I thought that moment of the night when Henry Grady stood among the curling wreaths of tobacco smoke in Delmonico's banquet-hall and said, 'I am a Cavalier among Roundheads.' . . . A ragged, ebony giant, squatted on the floor in one of the aisles, watched the orator with burning eyes and tremulous face until the supreme hour of applause came, and then the tears ran down his face. Most of the negroes in the audience were crying, perhaps without knowing just why."

Another notable occasion occurred in the year of Queen Victoria's Diamond Jubilee, when Booker Washington spoke at Boston in connection with the dedication of a monument erected to the memory of Colonel Robert Gould Shaw — 1837-1863 — who was killed at Fort Wagner while in command of the first coloured regiment which had been mustered to serve with the Northern Army. A Boston paper said: —

"The scene was full of historic beauty and deep significance. Rows and rows of people who are rarely seen at any public function, whole families of those who are certain to be out of town on a holiday, crowded the place to overflowing. The city was at her birthright *fête* in the persons of hundreds of her best citizens, men and women whose names and lives stand for the virtues that make for honourable, civic pride."

Some other similar scenes might be referred to; but in a general way Booker Washington does not value opportunities for platform service unless they tend to advance the cause of his great work at Tuskegee. Nor can this be wondered at when it is found that such service alone necessitates his being away from home during six months in each year. He married Miss Davidson, to whose efforts the Institute owed so much in its early days — in 1885; but this second Mrs Washington died about four years later, leaving two sons. The third wife of the Principal — married in 1893 — was a Miss Murray, who was trained at Fisk University.

The later developments of the work in its many departments at Tuskegee can best be realised by reference to certain recent numbers of the Institute's monthly paper, the *Southern Letter*.

We find that the school post-office is now recognised as part of the postal system of the country, and is responsible to the Government. A savings bank has been founded on the grounds to encourage thrift habits by receiving savings from teachers, students and coloured people living in the vicinity. This year a kindergarten teacher was to carry on a class in the new training school buildings. Last year (1901) agriculture was made a special feature; 4000 peach trees were planted, making a total of 5000 of this kind on the farm. "The students are not only taught how to plant and care for these trees, but are taught the principles of fruit-growing in all respects at the same time." There are fourteen young women in this division, and, like the others, they divide their time between the college classes and the farm: —

"They are ranked in their labour as they are in their recitations in the class-rooms. In the dairy they are not only getting instruction in theory, but are actually assisting in the care and use of the utensils, in which 120 gallons of milk are handled, twelve gallons of cream are ripened, and fifty pounds of butter are made each day. They are also making a comprehensive study of milk and its constituents, weeds and their harmful effects upon dairy products, general sanitation of dairy barns, the drawing of plans, etc. In the poultry division the young women put theory into practice by having individual responsibilities in the care of over 300 fowls. In this way they get actual experience in the sanitation of poultry houses, the care of runs and all the apparatus used, egg-testing, the use of insecticides, and the prevention and cure of fowl diseases. The increasing interest in fruit-growing all over the South makes it easy to interest the young women in horticulture. The school orchard of 5000 trees makes it possible to lay great stress on the practical side of fruit growing. Special attention is given to the quality and quantity of peaches, pears, apples and plums, figs, grapes and strawberries that can be grown in a home orchard. In the division of floriculture and landscape gardening a study of our common-door yards and the laying out and beautifying of same is required. The young women assist in the care of the school grounds by helping to trim and shape beds and borders and take care of shrubbery and flowers. One of the things the young women are very proud of is their market garden. They have helped to plan, and have done all the work in it this year (1901) except the ploughing. They have planned, laid out, prepared and planted their seed beds. They have also planned and constructed a cold frame-house, doing all the carpentry work themselves. They are required to keep an itemised account of the expenses incurred in raising and amounts realised from the sale of all vegetables. Although the young women have only been in this department two years, many good reports have come to us from communities where they have carried their improved ideas of these various lines of agriculture. To fully understand the need of this work, one must travel through the country districts and towns of the Southern States."

A Tuskegee negro Conference is held annually, and this year (1902) it assembled on February 19 and following day. Encouraging news from the distance is continually coming to hand. Thus, two graduates will be reported as getting on well in a town of Georgia. Then news comes to hand (December 1901) that the Tuskegee stall at the Charleston Exhibition attracted unusual attention. Even the Dark Continent itself comes in for some share of attention; for "we hear very encouraging reports from our students who went to West Africa to introduce the raising of cotton under the auspices of the German Government." We find Mrs Washington attending the meeting of the Coloured Women's Federation of Clubs at Vicksburg early in 1902, and no doubt she carried some rays of sunshine with her. The work, as a whole, is on a religious basis; and this fact is emphasised by such an announcement as that at Tuskegee "the Week of Prayer was observed with great profit and interest." It is important also to learn that the Nurse Training Department at Tuskegee is attracting more students than ever. It appears that both young men as well as young women are trained for this service; and a letter from one of the former, written in March 1902, from a town in Alabama, shows how former students become pioneers in the great work of uplifting their own race: —

"I am now at this place, and am Principal of a school which opened December 9 last year. We have bought and paid for fifteen acres of land, on which a two-storey building now stands. A part of the glass windows needed we have been able to put in. We are now preparing to build a dormitory on our grounds for our students next term. We shall be glad to have you send anything you can in the way of reading matter. We are trying to establish a library for the people of this community."

In some instances, as, for example, in Nashville, to which reference has been made, negroes are becoming prosperous men of business. In his monthly newspaper for February 1902, Booker Washington gave the picture of a large house of business owned by a coloured trader, and remarked: —

"While there are not many coloured people perhaps, as yet, who own such valuable pieces of property in the South, still there are many who are very fast approaching the point Mr —— has reached. Mr —— is not only a successful business man, having the respect and confidence of both races in Nashville, but he and his wife are leaders in religious and charitable work in the city of Nashville, and their home is a constant resort for those who represent all that is best and purest in the life of the negro race."

The following extract from a letter to Booker Washington from a white gentleman in the South (December 16, 1901), shows in what light even ex-planters themselves and their associates regard the work in progress: —

"Being more and more impressed with the importance of the favourable opportunity offered in this community for the educational uplift of your people, I am again prompted to write you and more fully explain the situation and the need of help to accomplish this important work. This community is densely populated with negroes — more than ten to one white person. The white people are moving to the towns. Thirty white persons in less than two years — none coming in — and negroes occupying the premises vacated. The few white people here are anxious to see the negro educated up to a higher standard of citizenship in morality, thrift and economy, as well as intellectual advancement. The negro school building is under way, but they have not the means to finish it, and nothing with which to furnish it, nor sufficient means to pay the teachers necessary for the school. I know of no community where the needed funds would be more appreciated or could possibly do more good for advancing the negroes' interest along educational lines."

Thus, no one can foresee whereunto the ever-developing work at Tuskegee may extend. The graduates, who are constantly going forth, become teachers and leaders among their own people; but, large as it is, the number trained is still too few.

CHAPTER X

VISIT TO EUROPE — RETURN TO TUSKEGEE

In the summer of the year 1899 Mr and Mrs Booker Washington had a sum of money given them by a number of friends, which was to be spent in making a tour in Europe. The travellers, after a prosperous voyage, landed at Antwerp and, after seeing something of Holland and France, came to England, where they were entertained by a number of friends.

On Monday, July 3, Dr and Mrs Brooke Herford gave a reception to meet Mr and Mrs Booker Washington, which took place at Essex Hall, Essex Street, Strand, and after this reception a meeting, at which a number of well-known and distinguished persons were present, also took place, and at which Mr J. H. Choate, the United States Ambassador, presided. The many who attended, and the quality of a large number, gave significance to this meeting, and testified in no equivocal manner to the esteem in which Booker Washington and his work were held in Great Britain. The following summary of the American Ambassador's speech on this occasion was given in *The Times*: —

> "The Chairman expressed the pleasure which he felt at having been asked to preside and to introduce to the meeting his friend, Mr Booker T. Washington. There were 10,000,000 coloured persons in the United States living side by side with some 60,000,000 of whites. The freedom of which the negroes had been deprived for more than 200 years had been restored to them, but the question was how best they could be enabled to take advantage of it. The blacks were an interesting race. Fidelity was their great characteristic. During the Civil War, when the South was stripped of every man and almost every boy to sustain their cause in arms, the women and children were left in the sole care, he might say, of these slaves, and no instance of violence or outrage that he had been able to learn was ever reported. He thought it would be admitted, therefore, that on that occasion they amply manifested their loyalty and fidelity to their masters. The black people had done much for themselves. About one-tenth of the men had acquired some portion of land, and they had made a certain advance. Mr Washington was a pupil of the late General Armstrong, who devoted many years of his life to the establishment and maintenance of the leading school at Hampton, Virginia. Mr Washington had qualified him-

self to follow in Armstrong's path. He also had founded a school, or training college, at Tuskegee, Alabama, where the pupils were not only given a primary education, but were afforded the means of earning a livelihood. There were now 1100 pupils in the school. About half the number of those who passed through it went out as teachers to spread the light and the knowledge they had acquired there among their own race, and the other half were put into a position to support themselves by manual trades. The Government of the United States thought well of the work. It gave the school a grant of 25,000 acres of land in Alabama only last year. The State of Alabama, in which it was placed, gave it an annual donation. In addition it derived something from the funds left by the great philanthropist, George Peabody, and from another fund founded by an American philanthropist. The remainder of the sum needed for carrying on the work — some £15,000 a year — was derived from voluntary contributions, which were stimulated by the appeals made by Mr Washington, whom he regarded as the leader of his race in America."

There were no long speeches at this reception and after meeting. Booker Washington himself was brief in his speech while describing the condition and outlook of the coloured race in the United States. He said: —

"Immediately after receiving their freedom the negroes, for the most part, got into debt, and they had not been able to free themselves to the present day. In many places it was found that as many as three-fourths of the coloured people were in debt, living on mortgaged land, and in many cases under agreements to pay interest on their indebtedness ranging between fifteen and forty per cent. The work of improving their condition was far from hopeless, and he was far from being discouraged. If his people got no other good out of slavery they got the habit of work. But they did not know how to utilise the results of their labour; the greatest injury which slavery wrought upon them was to deprive them of executive power, of the sense of independence. They required education and training, and this was gradually being provided. Starting in 1881 in the little town of Tuskegee with one teacher and thirty students, they had progressed until in the present day they had built up an institution which had connected with it over a thousand men and women. They had some eighty-six instructors, and in all that they did they tried to make a careful and honest study of the condition of the negroes and to advance their material and moral welfare. Industrial education was a vital power in helping to lift his people out of their present state. Twenty-six different industries were taught, and every student had to learn some trade or other in addition to the studies of the class-room. The coloured students came from upwards of twenty States and territories, and the labour which they performed had an economic value to the institution itself. There were thirty-eight buildings upon the grounds of the college, including a chapel having seating capacity for 2500 persons, built by the students themselves. The value of the entire property was about $300,000. Seeing that one-third of the population of the South was of the negro race, he held that no enterprise seeking the material, civil or moral welfare of America could disregard this element of the population and reach the highest good."

Mr Bryce, M.P., also gave a brief speech, and showed that he was in agreement with what the founder of the institution of Tuskegee had said in reference to the importance of basing the progress of the negroes on an industrial training: —

"Having made two or three visits to the South he had got an impression of the extreme complexity and difficulty of the problem which Mr Washington was so nobly striving to solve. It was no wonder that it should be difficult, seeing that the whites had such a long start of the coloured people in civilisation. He believed that the general sentiment of white people was one of friendliness and a desire to help the negroes. The exercise of political rights and the attainment to equal citizenship must depend upon the quality of the people who exercised those rights, and the best thing the coloured people could do, therefore, was to endeavour to attain material prosperity by making themselves capable of prosecuting these trades and occupations which they began to learn in the days of slavery, and which now, after waiting for twenty years, they had begun to see were necessary to their well-being."

At the present time the institution at Tuskegee represents a value of £100,000, if we include the endowment fund; and the annual cost of training 1100 or more students is not less than £16,000. The work continues to expand, as must ever be the case with all healthy enterprises of the kind. Perhaps the most hopeful symptom of all is the sanguine enthusiasm of Booker Washington himself, who, happily for himself and for those whom he seeks to benefit, is, and must ever be, an optimist. He believes that his race has a future, and that it is capable of being so uplifted as to become a benefit to the world. We must all allow that the right means are being used to bring about this new reformation; but, at the same time, we need not close our eyes to the fact that there are observers and even well-wishers of the coloured people who are not so hopeful. By way of giving what may be regarded as the more pessimistic view, take the following passage from an article in the *Daily Mail* of October 23, 1901: —

"Frederick Douglass was an honoured guest in hundreds of Northern homes; his career as United States senator was marked with every token of respect and admiration, and many others like him were expected to appear. But in the forty years since the war the North has become more conservative in this respect, although it has been untiring in its efforts to foster the negro's education, to direct his energy wisely, and to make him capable of enjoying the liberties of the American Republic. In the South there may still be oppression today and the restriction of the negro's constitutional rights, but such a charge has never been made against the North, even by the black man's most prejudiced apostles. If the North refuses toay to grant social equality to the negro, the reasons are that it is considered not only impossible to accomplish, but dangerous even to attempt. It is considered impossible because the feeling has deepened instead of being dispelled since the war, that the negro is greatly inferior by nature and will never be otherwise. In his forty years of freedom he has advanced more in crime and lawlessness, according to statistics, than he has in education or development. Taking the blacks and mulattos together they form sixteen percent. of the entire population, and furnish thirty percent. of the penitentiary convicts. Crimes against the person especially constitute a menace from the negro almost unknown before the war, and Frederick Douglass said, shortly before he died, 'It throws over every coloured man a mantle of odium, and sets upon him a mark for popular hatred more distressing than the mark set upon the first murderer. It has cooled our friends and fired our enemies.' The race has, as a matter of fact, shown almost no power to fight its own battles, and its problems hang like a weight of lead around the neck of the American people, a weight growing heavier and causing more hopelessness as the years go on."

If the above is not actually too dark a picture, the evil is certainly one which a great Republic need not regard as an evil incapable of correction. Booker Washington himself is not so sanguine as to ignore difficulties; he foresees clearly enough that the earlier half of this present century must needs be a time of much rough pioneering service on the part of those who are the most earnest friends of the negro race. As lookers-on from afar on the European side of the broad Atlantic, we are able to descry many reassuring signs. Both in the North and the South, Booker Washington has met with abundance of sympathy, and a good deal of honest, practical help. When Harvard University bestowed on him the degree of Master of Arts, he was the first negro who had ever received that distinction. That good Christian man and enlightened politician, the late President M'Kinley, paid a visit to Tuskegee at the end of 1899, and on behalf of the nation he was thankful for what was being done. His successor, President Roosevelt, entertained Booker Washington at dinner at the White House, thus showing that he was of the same mind as his predecessor. Thus the great work goes on from the beginning to the end of each year, the aim of the continued and far-reaching effort being to bring two races together, one being able to help the other because both have interests in common.

www.ingramcontent.com/pod-product-compliance
Lightning Source LLC
Chambersburg PA
CBHW031610040426
42452CB00006B/465